PSYCHOLOGY OF EMOTIONS, MOTIVATIONS AND ACTIONS

UNDERSTANDING IMPULSIVE BEHAVIOR

ASSESSMENT, INFLUENCES AND GENDER DIFFERENCES

Psychology of Emotions, Motivations and Actions

Additional books in this series can be found on Nova's website under the Series tab.

Additional e-books in this series can be found on Nova's website under the e-book tab.

PSYCHOLOGY OF EMOTIONS, MOTIVATIONS AND ACTIONS

UNDERSTANDING IMPULSIVE BEHAVIOR

ASSESSMENT, INFLUENCES AND GENDER DIFFERENCES

CHRISTIAN BRADDON
EDITOR

nova
science publishers
New York

Library of Congress Cataloging-in-Publication Data

ISBN: 978-1-53613-815-3

Published by Nova Science Publishers, Inc. † New York

CONTENTS

PREFACE

In this compilation, the authors begin by describing the main impulsive behavior assessment instruments in animals and humans. The following databases were searched from 2005 to 2017: MEDLINE, PsycINFO and BVS/Bireme. The search retrieved four questionnaires and eight tasks for humans, as well as six tasks for animals. This discussion, together with the analysis of instruments applied in human and non-human animals, is the greatest contribution to the field, since there is a lack of literature about the subject. In addition, this chapter discusses the importance of validating such instruments for each population. In the following chapter, the authors propose a developmental theory of persistence in problematic alcohol consumption that emanates from impulsigenic personality traits that differentially predispose individuals to drink when highly emotional. These patterns of behavior are reinforced over time and gradually shift from impulsive to compulsive, first to escape negative emotions, then to avoid them completely. For some, more adaptive methods of coping are not adequately developed. These individuals may transition into early adulthood far less equipped to cope with the stress related to this developmental period, and thus continue to drink in ways that are problematic and potentially harmful. The following chapter focuses on adolescence, a period of life wherein individuals pass through several changes, including experiencing new situations and new relationships with peers, parents and superiors. This phase of life is also marked by physical and brain maturation. The last area to develop in the central nervous system is the prefrontal cortex (PFC), the area also linked to the ability to control impulses. This suggests that adolescents tend to have more impulsive behaviors that can result in risky behaviors such as alcohol and drugs. So, the purpose of this chapter is to discuss impulsivity in adolescence, and clarify issues that may help us to understand topics related to this, such as the difference in impulsive behaviors between genders at this stage of life and what influence socioeconomic status may have on such behaviors. Afterwards, findings relating to emotional impulsiveness (EI) from the author's work and that of others are reviewed. Early work is first described that identified a neural (brain-wave) signature of EI in personality disordered offenders detained in high security. It was shown that, by categorizing offenders on the basis of this brain-wave measure as *a priori* high vs. low risk and following them up following their release into the community, it was possible to predict both general and violent re-offending with a modest degree of accuracy. Continuing, a review is included which summarizes the existing literature on the influence of the dimensions of impulsivity and alcohol use problems among racial/ethnic groups. In particular, the authors focus on how chronic stress may influence the relationship between specific dimensions of impulsivity (e.g., negative and positive urgency) and alcohol use. While much of the existing literature has been conducted in white samples, individuals from minority backgrounds often deal with greater stress and stress specifically related to their identity as minority. The authors go on to investigate the association between impulsive behaviors at age 7 and the development of problem gambling by adulthood. To determine the specificity of any observed association between impulsive behaviors and problem gambling, the chapter also examines the link between respondents' shy/depressed behaviors in childhood and later problem gambling. The longitudinal investigation found prospective evidence that impulsive behaviors at age 7 are a specific and significant risk factor for later problem gambling. In the concluding study, a total of 318 psychiatric patients from the outpatient services of two institutions and 184 healthy subjects were recruited. Patients were included if they were > 18 years of age, met DSM-

IV criteria for a psychotic, mood- or stress-related disorder and were clinically stable enough according to the treating physician to complete the study assessments. Healthy subjects were screened using the Structured Clinical Interview for DSM-IV (SCID-I) and were excluded if any diagnostic criteria was met or if they verbally reported a history of psychiatric disorders. The goal was to determine the impact of demographic variables and substance use in the overt expression of impulsivity in men and women with and without mental disorders.

Chapter 1 - The concept of impulsivity encompasses several behavioral dimensions, which result in complex and heterogeneous evaluation processes. To evaluate this construct it is essential the use of instruments that are valid and accurate. With this in mind, the objective of the present chapter was to describe the main impulsive behavior assessment instruments both in animals and humans, describing its positive and negative aspects. In addition, the authors discuss the differences between the use of scales and tasks for the evaluation of this construct, evaluating the pros and cons of each technique and the importance of validating such instruments for each population.

Chapter 2 - Most individuals decrease their drinking or "mature out" of problematic alcohol use following the college years into early adulthood. However, it is evident that a proportion of the population does not, instead persisting in problematic patterns of drinking behavior. Previous research and theory has cited social and role transitions that occur during this time to explain such stability and change in drinking patterns. Others have highlighted more complex processes involving changes in rates of new onset and recurrence versus rates of desistance. The authors propose a developmental theory of persistence in problematic alcohol consumption that emanates from impulsigenic personality traits that differentially predispose individuals to drink when highly emotional. These patterns of behavior are reinforced over time and gradually shift from impulsive to compulsive, first to escape negative emotions, then to avoid them completely. This maladaptive style of coping is likely masked during the college years, due to a widespread and normative culture of drinking. For some, more adaptive methods of coping are not adequately developed. These individuals may transition into early adulthood far less equipped to cope with the stress related to this developmental period, and thus continue to drink in ways that are problematic and potentially harmful. This theory has many clinical and public health implications. First, the authors may be able to identify individuals who are likely to persist and those who are not at a time when their drinking behaviors are largely the same. Further, the model provides direct opportunities for targeted intervention to prevent or moderate continued problematic drinking patterns into adulthood.

Chapter 3 - Adolescence is a period of life in which individuals pass through several changes, including experiencing new situations and new relationships with peers, parents, and superiors. This phase of life is also marked by physical and brain development. The last area to develop in the central nervous system is the prefrontal cortex (PFC), which is also linked to the ability to control impulses. This suggests that adolescents tend to have more impulsive behaviors than adults that can result in risky behaviors such as alcohol and drugs. This impulsivity can be characterized by cognitive and behavioral patterns which may lead to short- and long-term consequences. This impulsivity can be divided into three different dimensions: motor, attentional, and non-planning. Besides the discussion about impulsivity in adolescence, which may be associated with risk behaviors such as drug use, the socioeconomic status is relevant in this discussion as well, because studies found differences between socioeconomic status and executive functions in adolescents and preadolescents. Lower inhibitory control and lower performance in executive functions were related to childhood poverty. In addition, brain development occurs differently between boys and girls, which may result in differences in impulsivity between genders. So, the purpose of this chapter is to discuss impulsivity in adolescence and clarify issues that may help understand topics related to this, such as the difference in impulsive behaviors between genders at this stage of life and what influence socioeconomic status may have on such behaviors.

Chapter 4 - This chapter reviews findings relating to emotional impulsiveness (EI) from the author's work and that of others. Early work is first described that identified a neural (brain-wave) signature of EI in personality disordered offenders detained in high security. It was shown that, by categorizing offenders on the basis of this brain-wave measure as *a priori* high vs. low risk and following them up following their release into the community, it was possible to predict both general and violent re-offending with a modest degree of accuracy. More recent work is then described in which, in studies of personality disordered offenders, EI has been identified as a core feature of severe PD that, in part, accounts for the link between severe personality disorder and violence. It is suggested that, viewed through the lens of a hierarchical taxonomy of psychiatric disorder, EI represents a higher-order dimension that transcends particular psychiatric diagnoses and contributes to multiple forms of psychopathology. The studies reviewed herein concern male offenders, and further studies will be required to ascertain the extent to which the findings generalize to female offenders.

Chapter 5 - There is a robust relationship between impulsivity and alcohol use. The present review summarizes the existing literature on the influence of the dimensions of impulsivity and alcohol use problems among racial/ethnic groups. In particular, the authors focus on how chronic stress may influence the relationship between specific dimensions of impulsivity (e.g., negative and positive urgency) and alcohol use. While much of the existing literature has been conducted in White samples, individuals from minoritized backgrounds often deal with greater stress and stress specifically related to their identity as minority (e.g., minority stress). This unique source of stress may come from sources such as perceived discrimination and living in poverty, which exposes these individuals to additional stress and has a negative impact on substance use problems. In this chapter, the authors will integrate the literature on impulsivity, stress, and alcohol use in minoritized groups. The authors propose an organizing framework for how these constructs work together to increase alcohol-related problems in members from minoritized groups and discuss the implications of this research. Additionally, the authors suggest there is a strong need to develop unique treatment options that are culturally and developmentally appropriate, and that target each of these constructs for members from minoritized groups.

Chapter 6 - The authors prospectively investigated the association between impulsive behaviors at age 7 and the development of problem gambling by adulthood. To determine the specificity of any observed association between impulsive behaviors and problem gambling the authors also examined the link between respondents' shy/depressed behaviors in childhood and later problem gambling. Our study participants were 958 offspring of mothers enrolled in the Collaborative Perinatal Project who participated in an adult follow-up study at a mean age of 39 years. Multivariable logistic regression models were fit to determine associations between psychologist-rated impulsive and shy/depressed behaviors at age 7 and self-reported gambling as measured by the South Oaks Gambling Screen administered during the adult follow-up study. The authors found that children who exhibited impulsive behaviors at age 7, compared to their non-impulsive counterparts, were 3.24 (95% confidence interval: 1.47-7.14) times more likely to report problem gambling during adulthood. In contrast, the authors did not find a significant association between childhood shy/depressed behavior and problem gambling by adulthood in adjusted analyses. In conclusion, the authors' longitudinal investigation found prospective evidence that impulsive behaviors at age 7 are a specific and significant risk factor for later problem gambling.

Chapter 7 – *Introduction.* Impulsivity is defined as a predisposition toward unplanned reactions to stimuli. Its association with psychiatric disorders is not new since it has been considered a common clinical feature in several psychiatric diagnoses and a major predictor of substance use and attempted suicide. The construct of impulsivity encompasses various components, including personality, cognition and behavior and manifests differently across psychiatric disorders. One can therefore assume that there is not only an exclusive, one-way direction in the association between psychiatric disorders and impulsivity as the latter may influence the way impulsivity manifests. In addition, other variables such as gender and substance may also have a direct impact or act as moderators of impulsivity traits. Although evidence of the association between impulsivity, psychiatric disorders, substance abuse and certain individual characteristics such as gender exists, it remains unclear whether they contribute to increasing impulsivity traits, and whether this influence differs between men and women.

Objective. To determine the impact of demographic variables and substance use in the overt expression of impulsivity in men and women with and without mental disorders.

Method. A total of 318 psychiatric patients from the outpatient services of two institutions and 184 healthy subjects were recruited. Patients were included if they were ≥18 years of age, met DSM-IV criteria for a psychotic, mood- or stress-related disorder and were clinically stable enough according to the treating physician to complete the study assessments. Healthy subjects were screened using the Structured Clinical Interview for DSM-IV (SCID-I) and were excluded if any diagnostic criteria was met or if they verbally reported a history of psychiatric disorders. Demographic data and comorbidity with substance use were obtained from the patients' medical records and a direct clinical interview with all the respondents. Current use of alcohol, nicotine, cannabis and cocaine was recorded through a closed-ended (yes/no) question. Plutchik's Impulsivity Scale was used to assess impulsivity.

Results. A higher frequency of patients reported alcohol (40.4% vs. 29.3%, $p = 0.01$), cannabis (16.4% vs. 2.2%, $p < 0.001$), cocaine (9.3% vs. 1.1%, $p < 0.001$) and nicotine (29.6% vs.8.7%) use in comparison with healthy subjects. They were also more impulsive than healthy controls (22.5, S.D. = 7.5 vs. 13.7, S.D. = 6.6; $p < 0.001$) while women in the group of patients were more impulsive than men (23.5, S.D. = 7.4 vs. 20.1, S.D. = 7.1, $p = 0.002$). The presence of a psychiatric disorder and being younger were variables related to impulsivity in both men and women. However, other significant related variables were different by gender. In men, these variables were cocaine use, unemployment and being married; whereas in women they included alcohol use and lower educational attainment.

Conclusions. Impulsivity is present in patients with psychiatric disorders and the differences observed between them and healthy subjects can be at least partly explained by the younger age and correspondingly lower educational attainment reported in the clinical sample. In patients with psychiatric disorders, its manifestation may vary according to gender. According to various studies, this difference can be explained by the effects of hormones, but also by the different manifestation of impairments in cognitive performance and emotional regulation found between men and women. Our results for the association between substance use and impulsivity are consistent with previous research. However, the authors' findings highlight the way substance use has a different impact on impulsivity features by gender since frequency of use and motivations for use may differ between them. Despite its various limitations, the authors' study emphasizes the importance of the assessment of impulsivity in everyday clinical practice and the need for intervention strategies designed to reduce or manage its presence in a proactive way.

In: Understanding Impulsive Behavior ISBN: 978-1-53613-815-3
Editor: Christian Braddon

Chapter 1

Instruments and Limitations of Assessment of Impulsivity in Humans and Animals

Jonatas A. F. Passos, Alice Rodrigues Willhelm, Anderson Siqueira Pereira and Rosa Maria Martins de Almeida*

Laboratory of Psychology, Neuroscience and Behavior (LPNeC), Institute of Psychology – Universidade Federal do Rio Grande do Sul, Porto Alegre, RS, Brazil

Abstract

The concept of impulsivity encompasses several behavioral dimensions, which result in complex and heterogeneous evaluation processes. To evaluate this construct it is essential the use of instruments that are valid and accurate. With this in mind, the objective of the present chapter was to describe the main impulsive behavior assessment instruments both in animals and humans, describing its positive and negative aspects. In addition, we discuss the differences between the use

* Corresponding Author Email: rosa_almeida@yahoo.com.

of scales and tasks for the evaluation of this construct, evaluating the pros and cons of each technique and the importance of validating such instruments for each population.

INTRODUCTION

Impulsivity is a phenomenon related to different behaviors and cognitive processes, such as inhibitory control and reward discrimination (Humby & Wilkinson, 2011). In humans, impulsivity is defined as the "tendency to act spontaneously and without deliberation" (Carver, 2005, p. 313), so that the individuals do not consider the consequences of their acts (Araújo, Malloy-Diniz, & Rocha, 2009). It is a trait characterized by unplanned reactions before complete the process of information (LoBue et al., 2014). Sudden responses can manifest when the body has a low ability to inhibit behaviors that generate negative consequences, and often these responses are influenced by the individual's emotions and motivations (Casey & Jones, 2010; Torres et al., 2013).

Several studies have suggested an association between impulsivity and physical, psychological or material risk behaviors, such as reckless driving (Araújo et al., 2009), addictive behaviors (Lee, Storr, Ialongo, & Martins, 2011; Noël, Brevers, & Bechara, 2013; LoBue et al., 2014), unsafe sex (Cue Davis et al., 2013), violence (Cross, Copping, & Campbell, 2011), and self-injurious behavior (Ferrari, Harrison, & Lewis, 2012; Javdani, Sadeh, & Verona, 2011). These risk behaviors may often promote the association between impulsivity and increased mortality (Blonigen, Timko, Moos, & Moos, 2011; McGirr et al., 2008). Conversely, impulsivity may be important for survival when it is necessary to act quickly (Carver, 2005; Feist, 1998; Gullo & Dawe, 2008). In addition, a component of spontaneity is considered; for example, when someone answers what comes to mind or laughs at some joke at a dinner party, and creativity (Feist, 1998) (e.g.,: to bring a new subject into a casual conversation or create some new dish for a last minute dinner). The type of assessment used to evaluate dangerous behaviors and impulsivity varies from study to study and depends on the type of behavior to be observed. Many surveys use self-administered questionnaires to investigate behaviors (Lee et al., 2011; Willhelm et al., 2015; de Almeida et al., 2014). Moreover, animal and human research use behavioral tasks to evaluate participants (Lee et al., 2011; Wilhelm & Mitchell, 2008; 2012).

The concept of impulsivity is multifaceted (Ávila-Batista & Rueda, 2011; Cross et al., 2011), and there are various definitions and measures that are often interrelated (Brewer & Potenza, 2008; Green & Myerson, 2013; Perry & Carroll, 2008). Empirical research has mainly focused on two models of impulsivity, both in humans and animals: impulsive choice and impulsive act, or failure of inhibitory control (Leeman & Potenza, 2011; Mitchell, 2004; Perry & Carroll, 2008). Both types of impulsive behavior seem to have a mutual influence on each other by means of a two-way model, suggesting that the motivational circuits are connected to the inhibitory circuits, thus having an influence on each other (Casey & Jones, 2010; Hommer, Bjork, & Gilman, 2011).

Impulsive choice is one of the main manifestations of impulsivity both in humans and in animals and is related to motivational system (Adriani & Laviola, 2006; Cross et al., 2011; Odum, 2011). Therefore, impulsive individuals tend to choose smaller and immediate rewards or worse quality rewards, and they may not enjoy delayed rewards, even if they are larger and more interesting (Cardinal, Robbins, & Everitt, 2000; Perry & Carroll, 2008). Equally, impulsive individuals tend to choose the rewards they certainly will get, even if such rewards are smaller or less interesting (Myerson, Green, Scott Hanson, Holt, & Estle, 2003; Pupe, Brys, Asherson, & Bizarro, 2011).

Both types of impulsive behaviors may be associated. However, they have specific neural correlates that activate at the same time (Casey & Jones, 2010), which interferes in the choice of methods of psychological assessment. Prefrontal circuits tend to be more involved in inhibitory control (Humby & Wilkinson, 2011), whereas impulsive choice seems to be linked to several circuits of reward discrimination (Moreno et al., 2010; Valencia-Torres et al., 2012).

Impulsivity can be understood as either a state or a trait. The impulsive state consists of behavioral variation within a short period of time (Odum,

2011), and it may be influenced by several factors, such as the use of psychoactive substances (Olmstead, Hellemans, & Paine, 2006; Ortner, MacDonald, & Olmstead, 2003) or mood (Ansari & Derakshan, 2011), among others. The impulsive trait is a behavioral, emotional and affective pattern that is present over much of the individual's life cycle. Such a trait is manifested by a tendency to respond in certain ways within specific contexts (Brewer & Potenza, 2008). The impulsive trait includes a heterogeneous group of low-order traits, such as lack of premeditation, lack of perseverance, excessive risk behaviors, poor self-discipline, and sensation seeking (Cross et al., 2011). The assessment of impulsivity is generally focused on evaluating only trait or state, instead of both (Iribarren, Jiménez-Giménez, García-de Cecilia, & Rubio-Valladolid, 2011).

There are several measures of impulsive behavior because behavioral manifestations are quite diffused (Ávila-Batista & Rueda, 2011; Cross et al., 2011). The assessment of impulsivity has been investigated in recent reviews of the literature. Thus, the objective of chapter is to present and discuss the most used instruments that evaluate impulsivity in human and nonhuman animals, describing their characteristics, indications, and limitations. This discussion is based on translational research, which correlates basic research with animals and humans with clinical trials (Broos et al., 2012; Humby & Wilkinson, 2011). According to this paradigm, several research stages can be correlated through the translation of the results based on different models (Vivian et al., 2012).

Assessment in Human Models

Different manifestations of impulsivity, like motor impulsivity or attentional impulsivity are assessed using questionnaires and scales and/or behavioral tasks in studies with human participants (Ashare & Hawk, 2011; Mackillop et al., 2011; Whiteside & Lynam, 2001). Tasks as Delay Discounting and a Go/No-Go tend to focus on the impulsive state, whereas questionnaires are aimed at understanding impulsive traits (Cross et al., 2011; Iribarren et al., 2011). However, there are exceptions, such as a Delay

Discounting task adapted to assess trait (Odum, 2011; Tschernegg et al., 2015) and questionnaires developed to assess the impulsive state (Iribarren et al., 2011). The tasks can present measures of performance, time, number of errors, among others for the evaluation of a construct, for example impulsivity. They are usually administered by the evaluator and may have a higher cost, depending on the type of material your application requires. The questionnaires may be self-applicable, have lower costs and may be used in a variety of contexts, not only in research, clinics, hospitals, schools, and others.

QUESTIONNAIRES, INVENTORIES, AND SCALES

Questionnaires, inventories, and scales are standardized instruments containing several sentences. The participants must choose among the available options the one that best describes some of their specific characteristics. These assessment instruments are developed based on systematic processes of standardization and validation in various populations (Noronha & Vendramini, 2003).

The instrument most widely used worldwide is the latest version of the Barratt Impulsivity Scale (BIS-11). This scale assesses the pattern of impulsive trait based on three dimensions: cognitive (tendency to make quick decisions), motor (tendency to act suddenly), and planning denial (much greater interest in the present than in the future) (Ashare & Hawk, 2011).

The Sensation Seeking Scale (SSS) is a 40-item scale that assesses factors such as excitement, adventure seeking, experience seeking, and disinhibition (Marino et al., 2013). This scale makes it possible to investigate the relationship between impulsivity and risk behaviors, usually focused on sensation seeking (Roberti, Storch, & Bravata, 2003). Other scales are derived from other instruments or scales developed for specific populations. This is the case of the Impulsivity Assessment Scale (EsAvI, A and B formats), which was developed for the Brazilian reality (Ávila-Batista & Rueda, 2011). This 31-item scale is divided into four factors: lack of concentration and persistence, cognitive control, planning ahead, and recklessness and audacity. The items of both formats of the scale are compatible. Thus, the EsAvI can be administered twice to the same individual without a learning bias. While most scales tend to assess the impulsive trait, other scales, such as the State Impulsivity Scale (SIS), assess only the impulsive state (Iribarren et al., 2011). This scale consists of three factors: reward, automatism, and attentional response.

Tasks for Humans

Behavioral tasks assess mainly impulsive choice and inhibitory control. Many tasks use computer programs to store the individuals' answers or standardized tasks with specific material, like decks of cards. Some task used with humans can be seen in Table 1.

Impulsive choice is assessed using Delay Discounting and Probability Discounting protocols (Green & Myerson, 2013; Myerson et al., 2003; Tschernegg et al., 2015). The delay discounting protocol assumes that both impulsive and non-impulsive individuals tend to dislike delayed rewards, thus choosing short-term rewards instead of delayed rewards. However, this aversion is higher in impulsive individuals (Cardinal et al., 2000; Reed, Kaplan, & Brewer, 2012). The task consists of choosing between more immediate, smaller rewards and more delayed, but larger rewards.

The probability discounting protocol relates the impulsive choice to the aversion of the risk of not getting the reward (Green & Myerson, 2013). And the higher the risk, the lower the individuals' chance of choosing a larger reward. In both protocols, the size of the reward interferes with the result. If the reward is large enough, some individuals may choose to wait or face the risk of not getting the reward. The rewards can be real or hypothetical, and their results are often different if the discounting rate of the real reward is higher than that of the hypothetical reward (Lawyer, Schoepflin, Green, & Jenks, 2011; Smits, Stein, Johnson, Odum, & Madden, 2013) and depending on the characteristics of each reward, such as drugs, sex, food, or money (Lawyer & Schoepflin, 2013).

Table 1. Instruments and tasks to evaluate impulsivity in humans

Instrument	Kind of instrument	Aim	Relevant information
Stroop task (Golden, 1975)	Computerized task or manual task	The purpose of this test is to assess selective attention, the ability to maintain the goal in an activity, and inhibit the tendency to provide impulsive responses	The stoop task have several versions, among them with colors and letters. In addition, the versions encompass all ages, clinical groups and have different sizes.
Matching Familiar Figures Task (Egeland & Weinberg, 1976)	Manual Task	Aim to suggest measures of the reflection-impulsivity dimension	Usually used with children. It is a match-to-sample perceptual recognition task.
Wisconsin Card Sorting Test (Puente, 1985)	Computerized task or manual task	Aim to evaluate complex cognitive strategies, executive functions	Initially this test was created to evaluate people without difficulties or disabilities, but over time, variations have been launched to assess clinical population. Has already been considered a gold standard test for executive functions
Stop Signal Reaction Time (SSRT) (Logan, 1994)	Computerized task	It is a paradigm and the task measure inhibition of a response that has already been initiated, the ability to stop behavior	This task is also used in animal model experiments. With humans, it can have different configurations according to the demand, and can be used in clinical groups and at different ages
Barratt Impulsivity Scale (BIS-11) (Patton & Stanford, 1995)	Self-reported questionnaire	BIS is a questionnaire that intends to evaluate impulsivity in your three dimensions: attentional, motor and non-planning	The original one contains 30 questions, but has already been adapted for various countries, languages, age and sizes
Iowa Gambling Test (Bechara, Damasio, Tranel, & Damasio, 1997)	Computerized task	This instrument contemplates a decision-making situation, involving monetary choices, allowing to classify the decision-making behavior of the individual in averse or risk-seeking	This instrument has already been adapted for various clinical populations, age and countries and tends to always utilize monetization

Table 1. (Continued)

Instrument	Kind of instrument	Aim	Relevant information
Sensation Seeking Scale (SSS) (Zuckerman, 2007)	Self-reported questionnaire	Aim to investigate sensation seeking and four dimensions: Thrill and Adventure Seeking, Disinhibition, Experience Seeking and Boredom Susceptibility	It was created in 1964 by Marvin Zuckerman, but has been updated and has different versions, including scales that evaluate sexual sensation seeking
State Impulsivity Scale (SIS) (García-de Cecilia & Rubio-Valladolid, 2011)	Self-reported questionnaire	Aim to register and quantify impulsivity as "state."	This scale was designed based on three experimental models: Reward, Automatism and Attentional, and the questionnaire search the presence and frequency of impulsive behaviors
Delay Discounting task (Ortiz et al., 2015)	Computerized task	It is a paradigm and the task aims to investigate whether the individual reflects on bigger rewards in the future or more impulsive and immediate reward	This task usually involve money rewards and ask to participant chose a lower reward immediately or bigger reward in future
Go/No-Go (Willhelm, 2015)	Computerized task	It is a paradigm and the task requires a process of response selection between execution or inhibition of motor response triggered by a go or no-go stimulus	The task demands high level of cognitive functions of decision making, response selection and response inhibition. Several versions have already been standardized and marketed for healthy and clinical populations, ranging from pre-schoolers to adolescents

The Iowa Gambling Test, which follows the theoretical logic of the Probability Discounting test, is administered using cards that denote gain or loss of imaginary money values (Zhang et al., 2012). The individuals are instructed to maximize their gains removing cards from four decks that have distinct characteristics regarding reward and punishment (Takano, Takahashi, Tanaka, & Hironaka, 2010). The participants must choose the cards from the four decks until they get 100 cards, and they initially are unaware of the reward rule of the test: two decks have cards representing high short-term gain, but great risk of losing money over time, whereas the other two decks have cards with smaller rewards, with less chance of loss and greater gains in the long term (Tomassini et al., 2012). This test can be administered using either real cards or computers.

The tasks assessing inhibitory control measure the individual's ability to stop a certain behavior if an unwanted consequence may occur. These tasks usually involve other cognitive functions, such as attention, planning, and motor skills (Aichert et al., 2012; Dixon & Christoff, 2012). The impulsive act is assessed using various tasks, such as the Go/No-Go (GNG) and Stop Signal Reaction Time (SSRT) tasks (Humby & Wilkinson, 2011; Mulligan et al., 2011), as well as instruments from other psychological assessment batteries, such as the Wisconsin Card Sorting Test, although there is no consensus about its use (Steinmetz & Houssemand, 2011).

The GNG consists of showing a series of visual or auditory stimuli. When the individuals provide a positive response to some of these stimuli, they receive a reward (Go stimuli), whereas there is no reward and/or they get an aversive consequence (No-Go stimuli) for other positive responses, such as a shrill noise (Collins et al., 2012). The GNG is a virtual task and the stimuli are usually visual (Aichert et al., 2012; Rubia, Smith, & Taylor, 2007). The SSRT is a computer-based task that consists of showing several action stimuli. The difference between the GNG and the SSRT is that, in the SSRT, the individual must inhibit a certain behavior after its manifestation, whereas in the GNG the behavior did not happen (Aichert et al., 2012; Crosbie et al., 2013). The Immediate Memory Task is another task assessing inhibitory control and several other executive functions. In this test, the individual must identify the difference between a target number and other numbers, which may be similar or different from the target number. When the individual indicates that the similar number is the target number by mistake, this is considered to be a commission error. Impulsive individuals tend to have a high incidence of commission errors during the test (Dougherty et al., 2004). Finally, the Matching Familiar Figures Task assesses the impulsive act using the construct of reflection impulsivity, where the individual must identify possible solutions to a problem whose consequences are uncertain, measuring reaction time and errors: impulsive individuals respond faster and make more mistakes (Van Wel et al., 2012).

Assessment in Animals

Many tasks used in the assessment of impulsive behavior in humans are also adapted to animal research, such as Delay and Probability Discounting, Go/No-Go, and Stop Signal Reaction Time (SSRT) protocols (Broos et al., 2012; Cross et al., 2011; Perry & Carroll, 2008).

Animal research usually uses rodents as subjects in models that mimic different human conditions, such as ADHD (Fox, Hand, & Reilly, 2008; Puumala & Sirvio, 1998; Sontag, Tucha, Walitza, & Lange, 2010), substance abuse (Harty, Whaley, Halperin, & Ranaldi, 2011; Perry, Larson, German, Madden, & Carroll, 2005; Stanis, Burns, Sherrill, & Gulley, 2008; Wilhelm & Mitchell, 2008), or specific brain lesions possibly related to impulsivity (Kheramin et al., 2003; Mobini et al., 2002; Mobini, Chiang, Ho, Bradshaw, & Szabadi, 2000), based on the translational paradigm (Humby & Wilkinson, 2011). The main impulsivity models can be produced by inducing genetic changes and by means of pharmacological exposure (Sontag et al., 2010). Animal research use standardized behavioral tasks that assess mainly the two operational measures of impulsivity described above: impulsive choice, using the Delay Discounting protocol, and impulsive act, using various tasks such as the GNG, the Five Choice Serial Reaction Time Task (5CSRTT), and the SSRT (Perry & Carroll, 2008). These tasks are typically performed in operant boxes programmed with a specific protocol. The animals are conditioned with different rewards, such as sugar, food, alcohol, or other substances. Training in all tasks shares one thing in common: all of them start with a simpler procedure and become gradually more complex (Ghods-Sharifi, Onge, & Floresco, 2009; Harty et al., 2011). Training sessions may vary depending on the task and the reward involved (Calvert, Green, & Myerson, 2010).

In the Delay Discounting task, the animals must choose between two reward options: immediate, smaller reward and larger, delayed reward (Harty et al., 2011). After they make a choice, the animals must wait to collect the reward. The periods of time during which the animals must choose between the two options are called trial. After a certain number of trials, the animals go on to a new block, with different time for the reward to be delivered (Cardinal et al., 2000; Pupe et al., 2011).

Similarly to the task for humans, the Delay Discounting protocol for animals shares common characteristics with the Probability Discounting protocol (Ghods-Sharifi et al., 2009; Pupe et al., 2011). In this protocol, the animals must also choose between two types of rewards, a small, assured reward and a large, possible reward (Gilbert et al., 2011). Similarly to what happens in the protocol for humans, there is consensus that the Probability Discounting test is able to assess the impulsive choice in animals, although they may be correlated measures (Adriani & Laviola, 2006).

Both protocols generate data that can be understood using a hyperbolic equation (Ho, Mobini, Chiang, Bradshaw, & Szabadi, 1999; Pupe et al., 2011). Several baseline criteria have been described in the literature (Broos et al., 2012; Cardinal et al., 2000; Pupe et al., 2011; Wilhelm & Mitchell, 2012); however there is little consensus on what criterion is the most appropriate for each situation. The data analysis follows criteria similar to those of the analysis with humans (Broos et al., 2012). The rewards vary a lot, from sugar pellets (Cardinal et al., 2000; Torregrossa, Xie, & Taylor, 2012) to alcoholic drinks (Wilhelm & Mitchell, 2012) or other drugs (Koffarnus & Woods, 2011).

The GNG and SSRT tasks are similar in terms of execution because in both the animals must inhibit a specific response (Winstanley, 2011). In the GNG, the animals are conditioned to respond to a certain stimulus to receive the reward (Harrison, Everitt, & Robbins, 1999; Kolokotroni, Rodgers, &

Harrison, 2012). The stimulus is usually visual. When this stimulus is accompanied by another visual or auditory signal, the animals should not respond, otherwise they may not get the reward or receive a punishment, such as get trapped in a completely dark box (also called Time Out). In the SSRT, the animal perceives the response stimulus, but, in the presence of a visual or auditory signal, the response behavior, which is already underway, must be stopped, otherwise the reward may not be received or there might be a punishment (Bari et al., 2011; Eagle & Robbins, 2003).

Another task used to assess impulsivity used as a secondary measure is the Five Choice Serial Reaction Time (5CSRT) (Torregrossa et al., 2012). The main measure of this protocol is accuracy related to attention. In an operant box with five illuminated apertures, the animals must observe when the lights are turned on, and then poke their nose inside the aperture when the light inside is illuminated. If the animal responds correctly, it receives a reward. Premature responses before any of the five lights are illuminated characterized failure of inhibitory control, providing a measure of impulsivity in this activity (Sanchez-Roige, Peña-Oliver, & Stephens, 2012).

The Lever-Holding Task (LHT) is based on the differential reinforcement of low response rate (DLR) (Sanabria & Killeen, 2008). During the DLR procedure, the animal must issue a behavior, and wait for a certain time to repeat the same behavior so that there is reinforcement. Premature responses are considered impulsive, and reinforced responses within the given time and without significant delays are considered efficient. The LHT task is a DLR procedure in which the animal must press a bar for a certain period of time. If the animal let go off the bar before that period of time, the timer is restarted and the animal is not rewarded. Impulsive animals tend to let go off the bar before the specified period of time (Sanabria & Killeen, 2008).

Discussion about Assessments

The existence of various manifestations and concepts of impulsivity influences the existence of quite heterogeneous assessment methods (Broos et al., 2012; Torregrossa et al., 2012). The instruments assess similar concepts differently, but there are few studies trying to relate different tests (Baarendse & Vanderschuren, 2012; Broos et al., 2012; Kolokotroni, Rodgers, & Harrison, 2011). The difference between the assessment techniques, such as the use of computers, self-administered scales and behavioral tasks, should be taken into account because it may cause different results (Meda et al., 2009). Self-applicable scales may have biases related to social desirability, in which the research subject can respond from an image which he considers to be the most correct and unrelated to his own construct traits, and there is a possibility that subject does not have a realistic view of the presence or absence of the behavior asked in the scale in their repertoire of behaviors, making this type of instrument imprecise. The tasks, in turn, tend not to present this type of problem, since they evaluate the behavior itself, and not the subject's view about it, however, other variables such as physical disabilities can interfere in its execution. Another factor that must be taken into account is the cost-effectiveness of each type of evaluation. The scales tend to decrease the cost of the research, besides the possibility of being applied in a great number of subjects at the same time. Tasks tend to require computers or specific materials for their accomplishment, making the research more expensive.

Impulsivity may also be understood as a variation of the functioning of inhibitory and reward systems, which makes it possible to assess it using less specific tests that assess related constructs such as personality, attention, executive functions, among others (Cross et al., 2011; Romer et al., 2011; Stautz & Cooper, 2013; Steinmetz & Houssemand, 2011). However, impulsive behavior assumes importance because of the damage it may cause to both the impulsive individual (Blonigen et al., 2011) and to other people (Dvorak, Pearson, & Kuvaas, 2013). Thus, specific assessment methods may be more effective, although there are more tests used in research than in the clinical or diagnostic evaluation in several areas (Conselho Federal de Psicologia, 2013; Primi, 2010).

The response patterns found in the instruments are unique for each country, thus, the measures as averages, standard deviation, and standard error can vary from one population to another, so the instruments must be standardized and validated in each locality. The assessment of impulsive behavior must be adapted according to the population studied and the objectives of the evaluator (Broos et al., 2012; Malloy-Diniz et al., 2010). An instrument that is not validated may render data unreliable.

When it comes to assessing animals, the training process and the definition of baseline characteristics are as important as the data analysis. Training sessions organized according to increasing difficulty stages based on the behavioral paradigm is suitable for the implementation of a more streamlined and effective protocol (Foscue, Wood, & Schramm-Sapyta, 2012). The non-assumption of a standardized protocol in the training of animals may make it impossible to compare the data with other samples, as these data become unreliable. Therefore, it is imperative that, together with the tasks used for the evaluation, the steps necessary to train the animals in a research are taken into account.

The simultaneous administration of impulsivity tests may enhance the validation of the construct. Similarly to what may happen when there is an association with other close construct (Ávila-Batista & Rueda, 2011), such as aggressiveness, anxiety, or attention. The use of different instruments, such as self-administered scales and tasks, is also suggested (Cyders & Coskunpinar, 2011) because it promotes the understanding of the relationships between various manifestations of impulsive behavior. The association with instruments that assess similar measures, such as the Wisconsin Card Sorting Test (Steinmetz & Houssemand, 2011), scales of externalization (Carvalho, Patrick, Krueger, Markon, & Pinheiro, 2010), personality (Whiteside & Lynam, 2001), and executive functions (Betancourt et al., 2011) can promote understanding of the interaction between impulsive behavior and other functions.

Many instruments are common to both human subjects and animals, which is a characteristic of the translational research paradigm (Humby & Wilkinson, 2011). The translation between research with humans and animals should be encouraged because it promotes in-depth knowledge of impulsive behavior and other psychological processes. In addition, translational research allows researchers to perform interventions that are impossible to perform with humans for ethical reasons, such as observing the effects of brain injuries, drugs on the central nervous system, and even issues related to genetic changes. From the data of research of this nature with animals, it is possible to make a parallel of how these same conditions can affect humans. Gaining such knowledge is necessary to effectively develop medical technologies for different populations (Broos et al., 2012; Vivian et al., 2012). Caution should be taken when considering the individual characteristics of each species. And in terms of animal assessment, special attention should be given to different strains (Sousa, Almeida, & Wotjak, 2006); whereas the assessments of humans should consider cultural characteristics (Malloy-Diniz et al., 2010; Manzi-Oliveira, Balarini, Marques, & Pasian, 2011).

CONCLUSION

Impulsivity is a construct made up of many dimensions as well as cognitive and behavioral characteristics. There are several instruments that are able to measure facets of impulsive behavior, although a few instruments can measure different dimensions in a single test. Impulsivity assessment is often performed in research contexts, thus its clinical and diagnostic applicability should be investigated, given the importance of impulsive behavior in today's society.

This discussion, together with the analysis between instruments applied in human and non-human animals, is the greatest contribution of this review to the field, since there is a lack of literature about the subject. Standardized models and protocols for use in humans should be developed. This lack of standardization may impede to some degree the use of research results by other studies, including meta-analyses. In addition, it is important to discuss more about how research can approach the real world. Articles tend to bring important scientific insights, though it is necessary to be able to show the applicability of results in everyday life, like clinical practice. It is suggested that future reviews may bring this discussion to bear support professionals who can benefit with information about these instruments.

Finally, it is important to stress the importance of validating such instruments for each population. Further studies aimed at investigating particular characteristics of impulsive behavior are needed because of the cultural differences of each population group.

REFERENCES

Adriani, W., & Laviola, G. (2006). Delay aversion but preference for large and rare rewards in two choice tasks: implications for the measurement of self-control parameters. *BMC Neuroscience*, *7*, 11. doi: 1471-2202-7-52 [pii]10.1186/1471-2202-7-52.

Aichert, D. S., Wöstmann, N. M., Costa, A., Macare, C., Wenig, J. R., Möller, H. J., Rubia, K., et al., (2012). Associations between trait impulsivity and prepotent response inhibition. *Journal of clinical and experimental neuropsychology*, *34*(10), 1016–1032. doi: 10.1080/13803395.2012.706261.

Ansari, T. L., & Derakshan, N. (2011). The neural correlates of impaired inhibitory control in anxiety. *Neuropsychologia*, *49*(5), 1146–1153. doi: 10.1016/j.neuropsychologia.2011.01.019.

Araújo, M. M., Malloy-Diniz, L. F., & Rocha, F. L. (2009). Impulsiveness and traffic accidents. *Revista de psiquiatria clínica*, *36*(2), 60–68. doi: 10.1590/S0101-60832009000200004.

Ashare, R. L., & Hawk, L. W. (2011). Effects of smoking abstinence on impulsive behavior among smokers high and low in ADHD-like symptoms. *Psychopharmacology (Berlin)*. doi: 10.1007/s00213-011-2324-2.

Ávila-Batista, A. C., & Rueda, F. J. M. (2011). Construction and psychometric studies of an Impulsivity Assessment Scale. *Psico-USF*, *16*(3), 285–295. doi: 10.1590/S1413-82712011000300005.

Baarendse, P. J. J., & Vanderschuren, L. J. M. J. (2012). Dissociable effects of monoamine reuptake inhibitors on distinct forms of impulsive behavior in rats. *Psychopharmacology*, *219*(2), 313–326. doi: 10.1007/s00213-011-2576-x.

Bari, A., Mar, A. C., Theobald, D. E., Elands, S. A., Oganya, K. C., Eagle, D. M., & Robbins, T. W. (2011). Prefrontal and monoaminergic contributions to stop-signal task performance in rats. *The Journal of neuroscience*, *31*(25), 9254–9263. doi: 10.1523/JNEUROSCI.1543-11.2011.

Bechara, A., Damasio, H., Tranel, D., & Damasio, A. R. (2005). The Iowa Gambling Task and the somatic marker hypothesis: some questions and answers. *Trends in cognitive sciences*, *9*(4), 159–162.

Betancourt, L. M., Brodsky, N. L., Brown, C. A., McKenna, K. A., Giannetta, J. M., Yang, W., Romer, D., et al., (2011). Is Executive Cognitive Function Associated with Youth Gambling? *Journal of Gambling Studies*. doi: 10.1007/s10899-011-9256-y.

Blonigen, D. M., Timko, C., Moos, B. S., & Moos, R. H. (2011). Impulsivity Is an Independent Predictor of 15-Year Mortality Risk Among Individuals Seeking Help for Alcohol-Related Problems. *Alcoholism: Clinical and Experimental Research*, *35*(11), 11. doi: 10.1111/j.1530-0277.2011.01560.x.

Brewer, J. A., & Potenza, M. N. (2008). The neurobiology and genetics of impulse control disorders: relationships to drug addictions. *Biochemical Pharmacology*, *75*(1), 63–75. doi: 10.1016/j.bcp.2007.06.043.

Broos, N., Schmaal, L., Wiskerke, J., Kostelijk, L., Lam, T., Stoop, N., Weierink, L., et al., (2012). The Relationship between Impulsive Choice and Impulsive Action: A Cross-Species Translational Study. *PLoS ONE*, *7*(5). doi: 10.1371/journal.pone.0036781.

Calvert, A. L., Green, L., & Myerson, J. (2010). Delay discounting of qualitatively different reinforcers in rats. *Journal of the experimental analysis of behavior*, *93*(2), 171–184. doi: 10.1901/jeab.2010.93-171.

Cardinal, R. N., Robbins, T. W., & Everitt, B. J. (2000). The effects of d-amphetamine, chlordiazepoxide, alpha-flupenthixol and behavioural manipulations on choice of signalled and unsignalled delayed reinforcement in rats. *Psychopharmacology (Berlin)*, *152*(4), 362–75. doi: 10.1007/s002130000536.

Carvalho, H. W. de, Patrick, C. J., Krueger, R. F., Markon, K. E., & Pinheiro, Â. M. V. (2010). Construct validity of the Brazilian version of the

Externalizing Spectrum Inventory: evidence from a university student sample. *Revista de Psiquiatria Clínica, 37*(5), 206–211. doi: 10.1590/S0101-60832010000500004.

Carver, C. S. (2005). Impulse and constraint: perspectives from personality psychology, convergence with theory in other areas, and potential for integration. *Personality and Social Psychology Review*, *9*(4), 312–33. doi: 10.1207/s15327957pspr0904_2.

Casey, B. J., & Jones, R. M. (2010). Neurobiology of the adolescent brain and behavior: implications for substance use disorders. *Journal of the American Academy of Child & Adolescent Psychiatry*, *49*(12), 1189–201; quiz 1285. doi: S0890-8567(10)00670-2 [pii]10.1016/j.jaac.2010.08.017.

Cross, C. P., Copping, L. T., & Campbell, A. (2011). Sex differences in impulsivity: a meta-analysis. *Psychological Bulletin*, *137*(1), 97–130. doi: 2011-00025-004 [pii]10.1037/a0021591.

Collins, H. R., Corbly, C. R., Liu, X., Kelly, T. H., Lynam, D., & Joseph, J. E. (2012). Too little, too late or too much, too early? Differential hemodynamics of response inhibition in high and low sensation seekers. *Brain Research*, *1481*, 1–12. doi: 10.1016/j.brainres.2012.08.004.

Crosbie, J., Arnold, P., Paterson, A., Swanson, J., Dupuis, A., Li, X., Shan, J., et al., (2013). Response Inhibition and ADHD Traits: Correlates and Heritability in a Community Sample. *Journal of abnormal child psychology*. doi:10.1007/s10802-012-9693-9.

Conselho Federal de Psicologia. (2013, abril 24). Testes psicológicos aprovados para uso. *Sistema de Avaliação de Testes Psicológicos do Conselho Federal de Psicologia* [*Psychological tests approved for use. System of Evaluation of Psychological Tests of the Brazilian Federal Council of Psychology*]. Site do Conselho Federal de Psicologia, Accessed in april 24, 2013, http://www2.pol.org.br/satepsi/sistema/admin.cfm?lista1=sim.

Cue Davis, K., Stappenbeck, C. A., Norris, J., George, W. H., Jacques-Tiura, A. J., Schraufnagel, T. J., & Kajumulo, K. F. (2013). Young Men's Condom Use Resistance Tactics: A Latent Profile Analysis. *Journal of sex research*. doi: 10.1080/00224499.2013.776660.

Cyders, M. A., & Coskunpinar, A. (2011). Measurement of constructs using self-report and behavioral lab tasks: Is there overlap in nomothetic span and construct representation for impulsivity? *Clinical Psychology Review*, *31*(6), 965–982. doi: S0272-7358(11)00099-7[pii]10.1016/j.cpr.2011.06.001.

De Almeida, R. M. M. de, Trentini, L. B., Klein, L. A., Macuglia, G. R., Hammer, C., & Tesmmer, M. (2014). *Alcohol and Drugs Use, Levels of Impulsivity and Aggression in Adolescents in Rio Grande do Sul*. Psico, 45(1), 65–72. http://doi.org/10.15448/1980-8623.2014.1.12727.

Dixon, M. L., & Christoff, K. (2012). The Decision to Engage Cognitive Control Is Driven by Expected Reward-Value: Neural and Behavioral Evidence. *PLoS ONE*, *7*(12). doi: 10.1371/journal.pone.0051637.

Dougherty, D. M., Mathias, C. W., Marsh, D. M., Papageorgiou, T. D., Swann, A. C., & Moeller, F. G. (2004). Laboratory measured behavioral impulsivity relates to suicide attempt history. *Suicide and Life-Threatening Behavior*, *34*(4), 374–385. doi: 10.1521/suli.34.4.374.53738.

Dvorak, R. D., Pearson, M. R., & Kuvaas, N. J. (2013). The five-factor model of impulsivity-like traits and emotional lability in aggressive behavior. *Aggressive behavior*, *39*(3), 222–228. doi: 10.1002/ab.21474.

Eagle, D. M., & Robbins, T. W. (2003). Inhibitory control in rats performing a stop-signal reaction-time task: effects of lesions of the medial striatum and d-amphetamine. *Behavioral neuroscience*, *117*(6), 1302–1317. doi: 10.1037/0735-7044.117.6.1302.

Egeland, B., & Weinberg, R. A. (1976). The Matching Familiar Figures Test: A look at its psychometric credibility. *Child Development*, 483–491.

Feist, G. J. (1998). A meta-analysis of personality in scientific and artistic creativity. *Personality and Social Psychology Review*, *2*(4), 290–309. doi: 10.1207/s15327957pspr0204_5.

Ferrari, M., Harrison, B., & Lewis, D. (2012). The risk factors for impulsivity-related falls among hospitalized older adults. *Rehabilitation nursing: the official journal of the Association of Rehabilitation Nurses*, *37*(3), 145–150. doi: 10.1002/RNJ.00046.

Foscue, E. P., Wood, K. N., & Schramm-Sapyta, N. L. (2012). Characterization of a Semi-Rapid Method for Assessing Delay Discounting in Rodents. *Pharmacology, Biochemistry, and Behavior*, *101*(2), 187–192. doi: 10.1016/j.pbb.2012.01.006.

Fox, A. T., Hand, D. J., & Reilly, M. P. (2008). Impulsive choice in a rodent model of attention-deficit/hyperactivity disorder. *Behavioural Brain Research*, *187*(1), 146–52. doi: S0166-4328(07)00482-2[pii]10.1016/j.bbr.2007.09.008.

García-de Cecilia, J. M., & Rubio-Valladolid, G. (2011). Validation and psychometric properties of the State Impulsivity Scale (SIS). *Actas Esp Psiquiatr*, *39*(1), 49–60.

Ghods-Sharifi, S., Onge, J. R. S., & Floresco, S. B. (2009). Fundamental Contribution by the Basolateral Amygdala to Different Forms of Decision Making. *The Journal of Neuroscience*, *29*(16), 5251–5259. doi: 10.1523/JNEUROSCI.0315-09.2009.

Green, L., & Myerson, J. (2013). How Many Impulsivities? A Discounting Perspective. *Journal of the Experimental Analysis of Behavior*, *99*(1), 3–13. doi: 10.1002/jeab.1.

Golden, C. J. (1975). A group version of the Stroop Color and Word Test. *Journal of personality assessment*, *39*(4), 386–388.

Gullo, M. J., & Dawe, S. (2008). Impulsivity and adolescent substance use: rashly dismissed as "all-bad"? *Neuroscience and biobehavioral reviews*, *32*(8), 1507–1518. doi: 10.1016/j.neubiorev.2008.06.003.

Harrison, A. A., Everitt, B. J., & Robbins, T. W. (1999). Central serotonin depletion impairs both the acquisition and performance of a symmetrically reinforced go/no-go conditional visual discrimination. *Behavioural brain research*, *100*(1-2), 99–112.

Harty, S. C., Whaley, J. E., Halperin, J. M., & Ranaldi, R. (2011). Impulsive choice, as measured in a delay discounting paradigm, remains stable after chronic heroin administration. *Pharmacology Biochemistry and Behavior*, *98*(3), 337–40. doi: S0091-3057(11)00043-8[pii]10.1016/j.pbb.2011.02.004.

Ho, M. Y., Mobini, S., Chiang, T. J., Bradshaw, C. M., & Szabadi, E. (1999). Theory and method in the quantitative analysis of "impulsive choice" behaviour: implications for psychopharmacology. *Psychopharma-ocology*, *146*(4), 362–372.

Hommer, D. W., Bjork, J. M., & Gilman, J. M. (2011). Imaging brain response to reward in addictive disorders. *Annals of the New York Academy of Sciences*, *1216*, 50–61. doi: 10.1111/j.1749-6632.2010.05898.x.

Humby, T., & Wilkinson, L. S. (2011). Assaying dissociable elements of behavioural inhibition and impulsivity: translational utility of animal models. *Current Opinion in Pharmacology*, *11*(5), 534–539. doi: 10.1016/j.coph.2011.06.006.

Iribarren, M. M., Jiménez-Giménez, M., García-de Cecilia, J. M., & Rubio-Valladolid, G. (2011). Validation and psychometric properties of the State Impulsivity Scale (SIS). *Actas españolas de psiquiatría*, *39*(1), 49–60.

Javdani, S., Sadeh, N., & Verona, E. (2011). Suicidality as a function of impulsivity, callous-unemotional traits, and depressive symptoms in youth. *Journal of Abnormal Psychology*, *120*(2), 400–413. doi: 10.1037/a0021805.

Lawyer, S. R., & Schoepflin, F. J. (2013). Predicting domain-specific outcomes using delay and probability discounting for sexual versus monetary outcomes. *Behavioural processes*. doi: 10.1016/j.beproc.2013.03.001.

Logan, G. D. (1994). On the ability to inhibit thought and action: *A users' guide to the stop signal paradigm*.

Kheramin, S., Body, S., Ho, M., Velazquez-Martinez, D. N., Bradshaw, C. M., Szabadi, E., Deakin, J. F., et al., (2003). Role of the orbital prefrontal cortex in choice between delayed and uncertain reinforcers: a quantitative analysis. *Behavioural Processes*, *64*(3), 239–250. doi: S0376635703001426 [pii].

Kolokotroni, K. Z., Rodgers, R. J., & Harrison, A. A. (2011). Acute nicotine increases both impulsive choice and behavioural disinhibition in rats. *Psychopharmacology*, *217*(4), 455–473. doi: 10.1007/s00213-011-2296-2.

Kolokotroni, K. Z., Rodgers, R. J., & Harrison, A. A. (2012). Effects of chronic nicotine, nicotine withdrawal and subsequent nicotine challenges on behavioural inhibition in rats. *Psychopharmacology, 219*(2), 453–468. doi: 10.1007/s00213-011-2558-z.

Koffarnus, M. N., & Woods, J. H. (2011). Individual differences in discount rate are associated with demand for self-administered cocaine, but not sucrose. *Addiction biology*. doi: 10.1111/j.1369-1600.2011.00361.x.

Lee, G. P., Storr, C. L., Ialongo, N. S., & Martins, S. S. (2011). Compounded effect of early adolescence depressive symptoms and impulsivity on late adolescence gambling: a longitudinal study. *Journal of Adolescent Health, 48*(2), 164–9. doi: S1054-139X(10)00266-1 [pii]10.1016/ j.jadohealth.2010.06.002.

Leeman, R. F., & Potenza, M. N. (2011). Similarities and differences between pathological gambling and substance use disorders: a focus on impulsivity and compulsivity. *Psychopharmacology*. doi: 10.1007/ s00213-011-2550-7.

LoBue, C., Cullum, C. M., Braud, J., Walker, R., Winhusen, T., Suderajan, P., & Adinoff, B. (2014). Optimal neurocognitive, personality and behavioral measures for assessing impulsivity in cocaine dependence. *The American journal of drug and alcohol abuse, 40*(6), 455-462. doi: 10.3109/00952990.2014.939752.

Mackillop, J., Amlung, M. T., Few, L. R., Ray, L. A., Sweet, L. H., & Munafo, M. R. (2011). Delayed reward discounting and addictive behavior: a meta-analysis. *Psychopharmacology (Berlin), 216*(3), 305–21. doi: 10.1007/s00213-011-2229-0.

Malloy-Diniz, L. F., Mattos, P., Leite, W. B., Abreu, N., Coutinho, G., Paula, J. J. de, Tavares, H., et al., (2010). Translation and cultural adaptation of Barratt Impulsiveness Scale (BIS-11) for administration in Brazilian adults. *Jornal Brasileiro de Psiquiatria, 59*(2), 99–105. doi: 10.1590/S0047-20852010000200004.

Manzi-Oliveira, A. B., Balarini, F. B., Marques, L. A. da S., & Pasian, S. R. (2011). Cross-cultural adaptation of psychological assessment instruments: Brazilian literature review from 2000 to 2010. *Psico USF, 16*(3), 367–381.

Marino, E. N., Rosen, K. D., Gutierrez, A., Eckmann, M., Ramamurthy, S., & Potter, J. S. (2013). Impulsivity but not sensation seeking is associated with opioid analgesic misuse risk in patients with chronic pain. *Addictive Behaviors*, *38*(5), 2154–2157. doi: 10.1016/j.addbeh.2013. 01.020.

McGirr, A., Renaud, J., Bureau, A., Seguin, M., Lesage, A., & Turecki, G. (2008). Impulsive-aggressive behaviours and completed suicide across the life cycle: a predisposition for younger age of suicide. *Psychological medicine*, *38*(3), 407–417. doi: 10.1017/S0033291707001419.

Meda, S. A., Stevens, M. C., Potenza, M. N., Pittman, B., Gueorguieva, R., Andrews, M. M., Thomas, A. D., et al., (2009). Investigating the behavioral and self-report constructs of impulsivity domains using principal component analysis. *Behavioural Pharmacology*, *20*(5-6), 390–9. doi: 10.1097/FBP.0b013e32833113a3.

Mitchell, S. H. (2004). Measuring impulsivity and modeling its association with cigarette smoking. *Behavioral and Cognitive Neuroscience Reviews*, *3*(4), 261–275. doi: 10.1177/1534582305276838.

Mobini, S., Body, S., Ho, M. Y., Bradshaw, C. M., Szabadi, E., Deakin, J. F., & Anderson, I. M. (2002). Effects of lesions of the orbitofrontal cortex on sensitivity to delayed and probabilistic reinforcement. *Psychopharmacology (Berlin)*, *160*(3), 290–8. doi: 10.1007/s00213-001-0983-0.

Mobini, S., Chiang, T. J., Ho, M. Y., Bradshaw, C. M., & Szabadi, E. (2000). Effects of central 5-hydroxytryptamine depletion on sensitivity to delayed and probabilistic reinforcement. *Psychopharmacology (Berlin)*, *152*(4), 390–7.

Moreno, M., Cardona, D., Gomez, M. J., Sanchez-Santed, F., Tobena, A., Fernandez-Teruel, A., Campa, L., et al., (2010). Impulsivity characterization in the Roman high- and low-avoidance rat strains: behavioral and neurochemical differences. *Neuropsychopharmacology*, *35*(5), 1198–208. doi: npp2009224[pii]10.1038/npp.2009.224.

Mulligan, R. C., Knopik, V. S., Sweet, L. H., Fischer, M., Seidenberg, M., & Rao, S. M. (2011). Neural correlates of inhibitory control in adult

ADHD: Evidence from the Milwaukee longitudinal sample. *Psychiatry research*, *194*(2), 119–129. doi: 10.1016/j.pscychresns.2011.02.003.

Myerson, J., Green, L., Scott Hanson, J., Holt, D. D., & Estle, S. J. (2003). Discounting delayed and probabilistic rewards: Processes and traits. *Journal of Economic Psychology*, *24*(5), 619–635. doi: 10.1016/S0167-4870(03)00005-9.

Noël, X., Brevers, D., & Bechara, A. (2013). A neurocognitive approach to understanding the neurobiology of addiction. *Current opinion in neurobiology*. doi: 10.1016/j.conb.2013.01.018.

Noronha, A. P. P., & Vendramini, C. M. M. (2003). Psychometric parameters: comparative study between intelligence and personality tests. *Psicol. reflex. crit*, *16*(1), 177–182.

Odum, A. L. (2011). Delay discounting: trait variable? *Behavioural Processes*, *87*(1), 1–9. doi: S0376-6357(11)00036-2 [pii]10.1016/j. beproc. 2011.02.007.

Olmstead, M. C., Hellemans, K. G. C., & Paine, T. A. (2006). Alcohol-induced impulsivity in rats: an effect of cue salience? *Psychopharmacology*, *184*(2), 221–228. doi: 10.1007/s00213-005-0215-0.

Ortiz, N., Parsons, A., Whelan, R., Brennan, K., Agan, M. L., O'Connell, R.,…Garavan, H. (2015). Decreased frontal, striatal and cerebellar activation in adults with ADHD during an adaptive delay discounting task. *Acta Neurobiol. Exp. (Wars)*, *75*(3), 326–338.

Ortner, C. N. M., MacDonald, T. K., & Olmstead, M. C. (2003). Alcohol intoxication reduces impulsivity in the delay-discounting paradigm. *Alcohol and Alcoholism* (Oxford, Oxfordshire), *38*(2), 151–156.

Patton, J. H., & Stanford, M. S. (1995). Factor structure of the Barratt impulsiveness scale. *Journal of clinical psychology*, *51*(6), 768–774.

Perry, J. L., & Carroll, M. E. (2008). The role of impulsive behavior in drug abuse. *Psychopharmacology (Berlin)*, *200*(1), 1–26. doi: 0.1007/ s00213-008-1173-0.

Perry, J. L., Larson, E. B., German, J. P., Madden, G. J., & Carroll, M. E. (2005). Impulsivity (delay discounting) as a predictor of acquisition of

IV cocaine self-administration in female rats. *Psychopharmacology (Berlin)*, *178*(2-3), 193–201. doi: 10.1007/s00213-004-1994-4.

Primi, R. (2010). Psychological assessment in Brazil: foundations, current situation and future directions. *Psicologia: Teoria e Pesquisa*, *26*(25ANOS), 25 – 36.

Puente, A. (1985). Wisconsin card sorting test. *Test critiques*, *4*, 677–682.

Puumala, T., & Sirvio, J. (1998). Changes in activities of dopamine and serotonin systems in the frontal cortex underlie poor choice accuracy and impulsivity of rats in an attention task. *Neuroscience*, *83*(2), 489–99. doi: S0306452297003928 [pii].

Pupe, S., Brys, I., Asherson, P. J. E., & Bizarro, L. (2011). Prenatal alcohol exposure did not affect impulsivity in rats that performed delay or probability discounting tasks. *Psychology & Neuroscience*, *4*(1), 123–130. doi: 10.3922/j.psns.2011.1.014.

Reed, D. D., Kaplan, B. A., & Brewer, A. T. (2012). A tutorial on the use of Excel 2010 and Excel for Mac 2011 for conducting delay-discounting analyses. *Journal of Applied Behavior Analysis*, *45*(2), 375–386. doi: 10.1901/jaba.2012.45-375.

Roberti, J. W., Storch, E. A., & Bravata, E. (2003). Further psychometric support for the sensation seeking scale - Form V. *Journal of Personality Assessment*, *81*(3), 291–292. doi: 10.1207/S15327752JPA8103_12.

Romer, D., Betancourt, L. M., Brodsky, N. L., Giannetta, J. M., Yang, W., & Hurt, H. (2011). Does adolescent risk taking imply weak executive function? A prospective study of relations between working memory performance, impulsivity, and risk taking in early adolescence. *Developmental Science*, *14*(5), 1119–33. doi: 10.1111/j.1467-7687.2011.01061.x.

Rubia, K., Smith, A., & Taylor, E. (2007). Performance of children with attention deficit hyperactivity disorder (ADHD) on a test battery of impulsiveness. *Child Neuropsychology*, *13*(3), 276–304. doi: 10.1080/09297040600770761.

Sanabria, F., & Killeen, P. R. (2008). Evidence for impulsivity in the Spontaneously Hypertensive Rat drawn from complementary response-withholding tasks. *Behavioral and brain functions: BBF*, *4*, 7. doi: 10.1186/1744-9081-4-7.

Sanchez-Roige, S., Peña-Oliver, Y., & Stephens, D. (2012). Measuring impulsivity in mice: the five-choice serial reaction time task. *Psychopharmacology*, *219*(2), 253–270. doi: 10.1007/s00213-011-2560-5.

Smits, R. R., Stein, J. S., Johnson, P. S., Odum, A. L., & Madden, G. J. (2013). Test-retest reliability and construct validity of the Experiential Discounting Task. *Experimental and clinical psychopharmacology*, *21*(2), 155–163. doi: 10.1037/a0031725.

Sontag, T. A., Tucha, O., Walitza, S., & Lange, K. W. (2010). Animal models of attention deficit/hyperactivity disorder (ADHD): a critical review. *ADHD Attention Deficit and Hyperactivity Disorders*, *2*(1), 1–20. doi: 10.1007/s12402-010-0019-x.

Sousa, N., Almeida, O. F. X., & Wotjak, C. T. (2006). A hitchhiker's guide to behavioral analysis in laboratory rodents. *Genes, brain, and behavior*, *5 Suppl 2*, 5–24. doi: 10.1111/j.1601-183X.2006.00228.x.

Stanis, J. J., Burns, R. M., Sherrill, L. K., & Gulley, J. M. (2008). Disparate cocaine-induced locomotion as a predictor of choice behavior in rats trained in a delay-discounting task. *Drug and Alcohol Dependence*, *98*(1-2), 54–62. doi: S0376-8716(08)00163-4[pii]10.1016j.drugalcdep. 2008.04.009.

Stautz, K., & Cooper, A. (2013). Impulsivity-related personality traits and adolescent alcohol use: A meta-analytic review. *Clinical Psychology Review*, *33*(4), 574–592. doi: 10.1016/j.cpr.2013.03.003.

Steinmetz, J. P., & Houssemand, C. (2011). What about inhibition in the Wisconsin Card Sorting Test? *The Clinical neuropsychologist*, *25*(4), 652–669. doi: 10.1080/13854046.2011.568525.

Takano, Y., Takahashi, N., Tanaka, D., & Hironaka, N. (2010). Big Losses Lead to Irrational Decision-Making in Gambling Situations: Relationship between Deliberation and Impulsivity. *PLoS ONE*, *5*(2). doi: 10.1371/journal.pone.0009368.

Tomassini, A., Struglia, F., Spaziani, D., Pacifico, R., Stratta, P., & Rossi, A. (2012). Decision Making, Impulsivity, and Personality Traits in

Alcohol-Dependent Subjects. *The American Journal on Addictions*, *21*(3), 263–267. doi: 10.1111/j.1521-0391.2012.00225.x.

Torregrossa, M. M., Xie, M., & Taylor, J. R. (2012). Chronic corticosterone exposure during adolescence reduces impulsive action but increases impulsive choice and sensitivity to yohimbine in male Sprague-Dawley rats. *Neuropsychopharmacology: Official publication of the American College of Neuropsychopharmacology*, *37*(7), 1656–1670. doi: 10.1038/npp.2012.11.

Torres, A., Catena, A., Megías, A., Maldonado, A., Cándido, A., Verdejo-García, A., & Perales, J. C. (2013). Emotional and non-emotional pathways to impulsive behavior and addiction. *Frontiers in human neuroscience*, *7*, 43. doi: 10.3389/fnhum.2013.00043.

Tschernegg, M., Pletzer, B., Schwartenbeck, P., Ludersdorfer, P., Hoffmann, U., & Kronbichler, M. (2015). Impulsivity relates to striatal gray matter volumes in humans: evidence from a delay discounting paradigm. *Frontiers in human neuroscience, 9*, 384. doi: 10.3389/fnhum.2015.00384.

Valencia-Torres, L., Olarte-Sánchez, C. M., da Costa Araújo, S., Body, S., Bradshaw, C. M., & Szabadi, E. (2012). Nucleus accumbens and delay discounting in rats: evidence from a new quantitative protocol for analysing inter-temporal choice. *Psychopharmacology*, *219*(2), 271–283. doi: 10.1007/s00213-011-2459-1.

Van Wel, J. H. P., Kuypers, K. P. C., Theunissen, E. L., Bosker, W. M., Bakker, K., & Ramaekers, J. G. (2012). Effects of Acute MDMA Intoxication on Mood and Impulsivity: Role of the 5-HT2 and 5-HT1 Receptors. *PLoS ONE*, *7*(7). doi: 10.1371/journal.pone.0040187.

Vivian, D., Hershenberg, R., Teachman, B. A., G, A., Goldfried, M. R., & Wolfe, B. (2012). A translational model of research-practice integration. *Psychotherapy*, *49*(2), 143–151. doi: 10.1037/a0027925.

Whiteside, S. P., & Lynam, D. R. (2001). The Five Factor Model and impulsivity: using a structural model of personality to understand impulsivity. *Personality and Individual Differences*, *30*(4), 669–689. doi: 10.1016/S0191-8869(00)00064-7.

Wilhelm, C. J., & Mitchell, S. H. (2008). Rats bred for high alcohol drinking are more sensitive to delayed and probabilistic outcomes. *Genes, Brain and Behavior*, *7*(7), 705–13. doi: GBB406[pii]10.1111/j.1601-183X.2008.00406.x.

Wilhelm, C. J., & Mitchell, S. H. (2012). Acute Ethanol Does Not Always Affect Delay Discounting in Rats Selected to Prefer or Avoid Ethanol. *Alcohol and Alcoholism*, *47*(5), 518–524. doi: 10.1093/alcalc/ags059.

Willhelm, A. R. (2015). *Avaliação da impulsividade, controle inibitório e uso de álcool em pré-adolescentes e adolescentes*. [*Evaluation of impulsivity, inhibitory control and alcohol use in pre-adolescents and adolescents*]

Winstanley, C. A. (2011). The utility of rat models of impulsivity in developing pharmacotherapies for impulse control disorders. *British journal of pharmacology*, *164*(4), 1301–1321. doi: 10.1111/j.1476-5381.2011.01323.x.

Zhang, X. L., Wang, G. B., Zhao, L. Y., Sun, L. L., Wang, J., Wu, P., Lu, L., et al., (2012). Clonidine Improved Laboratory-Measured Decision-Making Performance in Abstinent Heroin Addicts. *PLoS ONE*, *7*(1). doi: 10.1371/journal.pone.0029084.

Zuckerman, M. (2007). The sensation seeking scale V (SSS-V): Still reliable and valid. *Personality and Individual Differences*, *43*(5), 1303–1305.

In: Understanding Impulsive Behavior
Editor: Christian Braddon
ISBN: 978-1-53613-815-3

Chapter 2

IMPULSIGENIC PERSONALITY TRAITS: FROM THE IMPULSIVE TO THE COMPULSIVE

Sarah J. Peterson*[*] *and Gregory T. Smith*[†]*, PhD
Department of Psychology, University of Kentucky,
Lexington, KY, US

ABSTRACT

Most individuals decrease their drinking or "mature out" of problematic alcohol use following the college years into early adulthood (Jochman & Fromme, 2010). However, it is evident that a proportion of the population does not, instead persisting in problematic patterns of drinking behavior (Jackson, Sher, Gotham, and Wood, 2001). Previous research and theory has cited social and role transitions that occur during this time to explain such stability and change in drinking patterns (e.g., Bachman et al., 2002). Others have highlighted more complex processes involving changes in rates of new onset and recurrence versus rates of desistance (Verges et al., 2012). We propose a developmental theory of persistence in problematic alcohol consumption that emanates from impulsigenic personality traits that differentially predispose individuals to

[*] Corresponding Author Email: sjpete2015@gmail.com.
[†] Corresponding Author Email: gsmith@email.uky.edu.

drink when highly emotional. These patterns of behavior are reinforced over time and gradually shift from impulsive to compulsive, first to escape negative emotions, then to avoid them completely. This maladaptive style of coping is likely masked during the college years, due to a widespread and normative culture of drinking (Sher, Bartholow, & Nanda, 2001; Slutske, 2005). For some, more adaptive methods of coping are not adequately developed. These individuals may transition into early adulthood far less equipped to cope with the stress related to this developmental period, and thus continue to drink in ways that are problematic and potentially harmful. This theory has many clinical and public health implications. First, we may be able to identify individuals who are likely to persist and those who are not at a time when their drinking behaviors are largely the same. Further, the model provides direct opportunities for targeted intervention to prevent or moderate continued problematic drinking patterns into adulthood.

INTRODUCTION

Alcohol consumption, in general, and problematic drinking, more specifically, have been shown to onset in adolescence, peak in early adulthood, and decline thereafter (Jochman & Fromme, 2010). One explanation for this phenomenon is the "maturing out" hypothesis, which suggests that emerging adults increase their drinking upon gaining new freedoms in the college years and decrease their drinking upon experiencing role transitions and gaining new responsibilities (i.e., employment, child-rearing, etc.) after graduation (Bachman O'Malley, & Johnston, 1981, 1984). This theory includes the observation that while most individuals mature out of their problematic drinking behaviors, as well as other substance use, a proportion of young adults do not (Jackson, Sher, Gotham, & Wood, 2001). These individuals appear to drink problematically past early adulthood, with many developing alcohol use disorder (AUD) following emerging adulthood.

A second, newer explanation proposed by Vergés and colleagues (2012) suggests that a "developmentally limited alcoholism" (Zucker, 1986, 1994) may not be so easily described. Utilizing data from the National Epidemiologic Survey on Alcohol and Related Conditions (NESARC), they found that although the 12-month prevalence of alcohol dependence (AD) decreased in emerging adulthood, patterns of stability and change in the persistence, recurrence, and new onset of AD are more complex. Specifically, reduced rates of AD in young adulthood may be due more to reduced rates of new onset and recurrence rather than increased rates of "maturing out," or offset.

There may prove to be an important distinction between meeting diagnostic criteria for AD, on the one hand, and drinking at problematic levels but below the diagnostic threshold, on the other hand. It does seem to be clear that there is reduced problem drinking overall among young adults, as compared to emerging adults/college age individuals (Verges et al., 2012). Because problems from drinking negatively affect individual health, relationship health, and overall productivity (Ellickson, Tucker, & Klein, 2003; Tucker, Orlando, & Ellickson, 2003), the study of reduced young adult drinking needs to consider both AD specifically and problem drinking more generally. Thus, it is important to develop and test theoretical models that explain which individuals are at risk to persist in problem drinking, including but not limited to AD, during the young adult years.

The collegiate years are an important time to examine problematic patterns of drinking, as they are a time of great change for many former high school students. These changes include increased freedom from parental control, increased autonomy, and increased availability of alcohol. In addition to these new contextual factors, there exists a widespread and normative culture of binge drinking on college campuses (Sher, Bartholow, & Nanda, 2001; Slutske, 2005). Approximately 60% of college students report drinking alcohol at least once a month, while two out of three of these individuals engage in binge drinking at least once a month (Hedden, 2015).

Drinking during the college years is associated with its own array of public health harms, including safety risks, sexual and physical assault, and even death (Hingson, Zha, & Weitzman, 2009; Hingson, Heeren, Winter & Wechsler, 2005). Another consequence of the drinking culture that exists on college campuses is the obscuration of potentially important differences between individuals, such as personality traits and skill deficits, that could discern which of these individuals are at a greater risk for persisting in their problematic alcohol use into the adult years. By drinking behavior alone, it is difficult to tell which youth will reduce their problem drinking when they take on the responsibilities of adulthood and which will not. Thus, individuals at risk to persist in problem drinking may miss out on a possible intervention and prevention period of great developmental importance. It is likely that some of these are the individuals who go on to develop AD. Further, it is plausible that this persistence is indicative of a larger problem, ultimately the failure to successfully transition into adult life.

The primary focus of this chapter is to elucidate a developmental model of persistence of problematic alcohol use that incorporates high-risk impulsigenic personality traits, psychosocial learning histories, and coping styles that are reinforced over childhood, adolescence, and emerging adulthood. We propose there is a pattern of development, characterized by elevations in personality and learning-based risk factors, together with deficits in developing adaptive strategies for coping with distress, that increases the probability that problem drinking will be maintained into adulthood. We argue that this pattern results in a gradual shift in which drinking behavior shifts from an impulsive act to a compulsive one, as these individuals likely enter adulthood ill-equipped to cope with difficult adult stressors and thus, come to depend on their past strategy of heavy episodic drinking. We expand upon the components of this developmental model below. Additionally, we discuss public health implications of this model, including possible assessment, prevention, and intervention efforts.

Persistence of Problematic Alcohol Use in Emerging Adulthood

Regardless of whether the maturing out phenomenon is as widespread as once believed, there is evidence that a proportion of young adults do persist in heavy, problematic drinking (e.g., Jackson et al., 2001). Gotham, Sher & Wood (1997) found that broad Five Factor Model (FFM) traits as measured by the NEO (Costa & McCrae, 1992) predicted patterns of frequent intoxication three years following college graduation. Openness, agreeableness, and conscientiousness all played a role, but only openness to experiences was predictive prospectively. This study pointed to the importance of individual-difference variables in the prediction of drinking behavior across the transition from college into adulthood. Others have continued to examine individual difference variables such as personality traits (Gates, Corbin & Fromme, 2016; Jackson & Sher, 2005; Littlefield, Sher & Wood, 2009; Rutledge & Sher, 2001), drinking motives, and expectancies (Rutledge & Sher, 2001; Jackson & Sher, 2005; Littlefield et al., 2009; Littlefield, Verges, Rosinski, Steinley & Sher, 2013).

The focus by these authors on individual difference factors is important. Given previous issues with differentiating these individuals on drinking behavior and diagnostic criteria alone, the key to identifying individuals who persist may lie with individual difference measures. Further, it may prove valuable to identify persons at risk for persisting in problem drinking in adulthood. Identification of high-risk individuals would make it possible to provide prevention and intervention efforts before, or shortly after, problem drinking behavior has begun. To the degree that persistence in problem drinking in young adulthood reflects broader developmental difficulties with making the transition to adulthood, it may be useful to provide skill training in making that transition prior to adulthood. This suggests the importance of identifying specific risk factors for persistent problematic alcohol use and applying them to assessment, prevention, and intervention efforts during the college years, as opposed to waiting to discover which students go on to transition successfully into young adulthood and which continue to consume alcohol in a problematic manner.

A Developmental Model of Persistence

Our theory holds that high-risk impulsigenic traits, psychosocial learning histories regarding the rewarding effects of alcohol consumption, and preferred coping style each play a role in the prediction of persistent problematic alcohol use. Beyond their singular effects, this theory also posits that these factors transact to create an overall model of risk for this process. We provide rationale and evidence for each of these risk factors and their transaction below.

Impulsigenic Traits

Many models exist to describe the role that personality traits play in risk for alcoholism and problematic drinking. (Birkley & Smith, 2011; Sher & Trull, 1994; Wills, Sandy, Yaeger, Cleary & Shinar, 2001). One such model, developed by Whiteside and Lynam (2001) and Cyders and Smith (2007, 2008a), identifies three personality traits that increase risk for impulsive behavior. Both theoretically and empirically, these traits appear to reflect different personality pathways toward addictive behavior. One trait is called urgency, with positive and negative facets. (Cyders & Smith, 2007, 2008a). Positive and negative urgency reflect the tendencies to act rashly when experiencing very positive and very negative emotion, respectively. The second trait is low conscientiousness. It also has two facets: lack of planning (the tendency to act without forethought) and lack of perseverance (difficulty maintaining a focus on tasks). The third trait is sensation seeking, which reflects a disposition to seek out novel, thrilling stimulation (Whiteside & Lynam, 2001; Cyders & Smith, 2007). Empirically, these three traits share from less than 1% to 13% of their variance (Gunn & Smith, 2010; Cyders & Smith, 2007). Each of these traits relates both concurrently and prospectively to problematic patterns of drinking (Cyders, Flory, Rainer & Smith, 2009; Guller, Zapolski, & Smith, 2015a; Peterson, Davis, & Smith, in press; Peterson & Smith, 2017; Settles, Zapolski, & Smith, 2014).

Positive and negative urgency can be conceptualized as distinct from the other five traits as they are affect-based. They entail a tendency to behave rashly when highly emotional. Neither sensation seeking nor the two low conscientiousness traits (lack of planning and lack of perseverance) are based on affective arousal. Thus, urgency and its facets have been thought to be particularly important in the risk process for addictive behavior, including problematic alcohol use. As such, they are also likely to be particularly important in the prediction of persistent problematic drinking.

In collegiate populations, urgency has been shown to predict future alcohol use and problems experienced after drinking, such as blackouts, hangovers, trouble with the law, or getting into fights. Cyders et al. (2009) found that positive urgency prospectively predicted increases in the quantity of alcohol consumed and the resulting negative outcomes experienced by college students. Similarly, positive and negative urgency predicted drinking quantity prospectively in first year college students (Settles, Cyders, & Smith, 2010). Experimentally, Cyders, Flory, Rainer, and Smith (2010) found that positive urgency significantly predicted negative outcomes on a risk-taking task and increases in beer consumption following a positive mood manipulation. Multiple meta-analytic reviews of impulsivity-related traits have shown negative urgency to have the greatest association with addictive behavior involvement (Berg, Latzman, Bliwise, & Lilienfeld, 2015; Coskunpinar, Dir, & Cyders, 2013; Fischer, Smith & Cyders, 2008; Stautz & Cooper, 2013). Given this, it follows that individuals higher in urgency may also be more likely to continue to binge drink past the collegiate years.

It is possible that positive and negative urgency may play different roles in the risk process. Among emerging adults, positive urgency appears to lead to increased drinking due to its impact on expectancies about the positive and arousing effects of alcohol, whereas negative urgency leads to increased drinking due to its influence on motives to cope with subjective distress (Settles et al., 2010). The difference between the two traits may be valuable for understanding who persists in problematic alcohol use into adulthood. Perhaps it is the case that negative urgency, rather than positive urgency, plays a stronger role in persistence. As individuals leave college, there is perhaps less of a culture of "partying" and celebration where positive arousal is normative, making positive urgency less impactful on the decision to consume alcohol. However, stressors and responsibilities increase following the collegiate years and it may be more likely that individuals consume alcohol to combat the emotional aftereffects of dealing with occupational or familial stress. If so, the disposition to act rashly when distressed, negative urgency, may play more of a role in problem drinking persistence.

Urgency may also play an important role in persistence due to its reciprocal relationship with drinking over time. Past research has documented a reciprocal predictive process between early drinking behavior and urgency levels among youth (Riley, Rukavina, & Smith, 2016), such that each predicts increases in the other over time. Over time, just as drinking itself is reinforced through reduction of negative and enhancement of positive moods, the disposition to engage in drinking may be reinforced, leading to gradual increases in that disposition, i.e., in urgency. It is also the case that among college students, problem drinking has been shown to predict subsequent increases in negative urgency (Kaiser, Davis, Milich, Smith, & Charnigo, in press). Thus, it seems likely that individuals high in urgency who engage in problematic drinking enter a negative feedback loop, which may ultimately lead them to persist in their patterns of dysfunctional alcohol use.

To date, there have been no tests of our hypothesis that urgency plays a role in explaining problem drinking persistence into adulthood. Prior studies have focused on impulsivity more generally or broader constructs such as "behavioral dyscontrol". An important next step is to test the urgency hypothesis.

As useful as personality traits have been for understanding drinking risk, traits are broad constructs that describe general behavioral dispositions. Nothing about being elevated on a given trait, such as urgency, explains an individual's specific behavioral choice to drink heavily. To explain such a choice, it is necessary to introduce an additional component in our risk model. We propose that psychosocial learning related to drinking, i.e., learning through experience and modeling to expect reinforcement from drinking behavior, plays an important role in understanding problem drinking persistence. In the following section, we introduce this second significant component of our theory, psychosocial learning as measured by expectancies.

Learning

There are multiple models concerning learned expectancies relating behaviors to outcomes. In the model we use, expectancies serve as markers of memory-based associative learning (Goldman, Darkes & DelBoca, 1999; Goldman, Reich & Darkes, 2006). They represent summaries of one's learning history about the outcomes of behavior choices and anticipated reinforcement from those behaviors (Bolles, 1972; Peterson & Smith, 2016; Tolman, 1932); these associations influence one's behavior in the future. This model assigns less weight to deliberative action (see Ajzen & Fishbein, 1980, for such a model) and more to learned associations of a behavior (such as drinking) and a reward (such as positive social experience). The association influences the behavior (Bolles, 1972; Tolman, 1932), and one may or may not experience oneself as choosing the behavior explicitly to obtain the expected outcome. Expectancies can form through both direct experience and modeling (Miller, Smith & Goldman, 1990; Zucker, Kincaid, Fitzgerald, & Bingham, 1995). Empirical support for this expectancy model has accrued over several decades (Bolles, 1972; Brandon & Baker, 1991; Doran et al., 2013; Goldman, Brown, Christiansen, & Smith, 1991; Lewis-Esquerre, Rodrigue & Kahler, 2005; Pearson, Combs, Zapolski, & Smith, 2012; Peterson et al., in press; Rotter, 1975, Tolman, 1932).

Prospectively, expectancies for reinforcement from drinking predict the onset of, and increases in, drinking frequency, quantity, and drinking-related problems (Goldberg, Halpern-Felsher, & Millstein, 2002; Ouellette, Gerrard, Gibbons, & Reis-Bergan, 1999; Peterson et al., in press; Settles et al., 2014; Smith, Goldman, Greenbaum, & Christiansen, 1995). An experimental reduction in expectancies for reinforcement from drinking produced drinking reductions compared to controls (Lau-Barraco & Dunn, 2008; Darkes & Goldman, 1993). Identified reinforcing effects from drinking include social facilitation and the regulation of negative affect. Thus it seems likely that greater expectancies would make one more likely to persist in their patterns of problematic alcohol use after the collegiate years.

Just as with urgency, there also appears to exist a reciprocal relationship between alcohol expectancies and drinking behavior. In adolescence, research on two longitudinal samples has shown that (a) drinking behavior does predict subsequent expectancies, controlling for prior expectancies; and (b) that prediction is positive, such that drinking experience leads to further increases in expectancies for reinforcement from drinking (Settles et al., 2014; Smith et al., 1995). Thus, there is replicated evidence for a reciprocal relationship, in the form of a positive feedback loop, between alcohol expectancies and adolescent drinking behavior. Expected reinforcement from drinking predicts both the onset of and increases in drinking behavior, which predicts subsequent increases in positive expectancies of drinking, which in turn predict further increases in drinking.

Similarly to the feedback loop between urgency and drinking, the feedback loop between expectancies and drinking behavior may function in early adulthood to enhance persistence of problematic drinking behaviors. As individuals go through college they may learn that when they experience a negative emotion, drinking mitigates that experience. Because there appears to be a positive feedback loop during adolescence, with no evidence of an interruption in that process over time, it seems likely that elevations in alcohol expectancies continue to predict problem drinking and thus persistence in problem drinking over time.

Coping

Stress is a normal part of any individual's life. However, there are specific stressors related to the college years and emerging adulthood in general. College students must now function as adults independently, with lessened parental support. They are faced with many important decision regarding schooling and career. Further, upon leaving college, these individuals must navigate the adult world of independence, responsibility for the self, employment, and potentially marriage and child-rearing. The way an individual copes with these stressors can influence outcomes for that individual. Research shows that coping style mediates the relationship between antecedent stressors and psychological outcomes (Compas. Connor-Smith, Saltzman, Thomsen, & Wadsworth, 2001; Wills et al., 2001). Coping has been conceptualized as a multidimensional construct reflected in the tendency a) to behaviorally or cognitively address the distress or b) to quell the emotional response to the distress. These have been referred to as task-oriented (or problem-focused) coping and emotion-focused coping, respectively (Carver, Scheier, & Weintraub, 1989).

Several studies have examined the relationship between coping style and outcome behaviors. Emotion-oriented coping is consistently associated with several maladaptive outcomes in adolescents, including greater affective, behavioral and social dysfunction (Compas, Malcarne, & Fondacaro, 1988; Windle & Windle, 1996). More specifically, emotionally related coping strategies in seventh graders predicted higher levels of substance use in eighth and ninth grade, whereas behavior (task–oriented) coping predicted less substance use in eighth and ninth grades (Wills et al., 2001). Emotion-oriented coping has also been found to be associated with depression (Bruder-Mattson & Hovanitz, 1990), suicidality (Edwards & Holden, 2001) and eating problems (Loumidis & Wells, 2001; Spoor, Bekker, Van Strien, & van Heck, 2007; Koff & Sangani, 1997). Conversely, task-oriented coping (or problem-focused) has been shown to negatively relate to many of these problems, including depression and anxiety (Glyshaw, Cohen, & Towbes, 1989) and behavioral dysfunction (Dubow & Tisak, 1989; Dubow, Tisak, Causey, Hryshko, Reid, 1991). Task-oriented coping was also positively associated with GPA (Rafnsson, Jonsson & Windle, 2006; Windle & Windle, 1996).

Preliminary research has also suggested that coping style development is a function of multiple factors, including personality. Cole, Peterson, and Smith (2018) found that urgency and low conscientiousness predicted coping styles in an adolescent sample such that higher levels of these traits accounted for more emotion-oriented coping and less task-oriented coping. This model is in line with urgency theory, which suggests that impulsive action, such as binge drinking behavior, for those with high levels of the trait serves an emotion-oriented purpose. These actions distract from distress or heighten positive mood (Cyders & Smith, 2008a). For many, problematic alcohol consumption may quell feelings of distress, providing short-term relief despite its long-term harms. Drinking to manage distress is directly at odds with task-oriented styles, in which the source of distress is identified and dealt with either behaviorally or cognitively.

From this framework, it follows that coping style is likely to play a role in persistence of binge drinking. Each time a highly urgent individual consumes alcohol to alleviate distress, that individual misses an opportunity to respond to the distress in a problem-focused way (i.e., focusing on solving the problem that led to the distress). Because behaviors such as alcohol consumption provide immediate reinforcement, emotion-oriented coping is reinforced and task-focused coping is not learned. Thus, individuals high in negative urgency are less likely to develop task-oriented coping skills (Cole et al., 2018). Upon leaving college, the stressors and sources of distress become more serious (i.e., gaining employment, occupational attainment, financial decisions, marriage and child-rearing, etc.), necessitating effective coping strategies. Individuals who cope with distress in emotion-oriented ways (i.e., consuming alcohol) are likely to continue to use such strategies in adulthood.

Transactional Process: Impulsive to Compulsive

While each of the above factors has been shown empirically to predict alcohol use in adolescence and early adulthood, it has also been theorized that transactions between these risk factors also influence one's addictive behavior involvement. The Acquired Preparedness (AP) model of risk holds that variation in personality can lead different people to experience objectively similar events differently. As a result, two individuals can learn different things and form different expectancies from similar events due to differences in their personalities (Davis, Riley, & Smith, in press; Smith, Williams, Fister, Cyders, & Kelley, 2006). Thus, although psychosocial learning is a product of experience, it may also be shaped in part by one's personality. With respect to dysfunction, high-risk personality traits can contribute to the formation of high-risk expectancies, thus increasing risk for maladaptive behavior (Davis et al., in press).

The AP model has received consistent empirical support in the form of longitudinal studies in which expectancy change mediates the predictive influence of prior personality on subsequent behavior. The model has been supported with respect to the prediction of drinking in both young adults (Corbin, Iwamoto, & Fromme, 2011; Settles et al., 2010) and in youth making the transition to middle school and high school (Settles et al., 2014; Peterson et al., in press). In these studies, the initial personality traits tested included urgency, sensation seeking, and low conscientiousness. Peterson et al. (in press) found that patterns of drinking in adolescence could be predicted by urgency and expectancies such that these variables and their transaction differentiated trajectory groups before drinking behavior began. In addition, they found that adolescents who began drinking early (prior to fifth grade) exhibited the highest levels of urgency, sensation seeking, and expectancies regarding social facilitation. This work suggests that the AP model is predictive of not only the level of alcohol consumption, but also the pattern of use an individual is likely to follow.

In clinical field research, the AP model has been shown to be applicable to risk for problematic drinking behavior in college students. Settles et al. (2010) found two AP pathways in their three-wave study of first year college students. The trait of positive urgency predicted increased expectancies for positive arousing effects of alcohol over time, and in turn this expectancy predicted subsequent increases in drinking quantity. The trait of negative urgency predicted increases in the motive to drink to cope with distress, which in part reflects the expectancy that drinking does help one manage distress, and the motive in turn predicted subsequent increases in drinking quantity. Also with college students, expectancies for reinforcement from drinking mediated the predictive influence of trait disinhibition (measured as sensation seeking, novelty seeking, and lack of planning) on drinking behavior over a four year period (Corbin et al., 2011) and the predictive influence of a trait reflecting the inclination to act in pursuit of reward (the behavioral activation system) on drinking over a three year period (Wardell, Read, Colder, & Merrill, 2012). These latter two findings suggest that the

AP process is likely to operate for multiple impulsivity-related personality traits, not just for the urgency traits.

The AP model can easily be extended to include coping, as the variables in this model have been shown to predict individual coping styles. As highlighted above, urgency theory suggests that highly urgent individuals are more likely to engage in emotion-oriented coping, such as drinking to quell distress, than task-oriented coping (Cole et al., 2018). Thus, just as high-risk personality traits anticipate the development of high-risk alcohol expectancies, so they anticipate the development of maladaptive coping styles. A comprehensive model of individual difference risk factors for persistence of problem drinking can be seen to incorporate personality, learning, and coping styles.

Importantly, the relationship between many of these variables has been shown to be reciprocal in nature, such that elevations in one lead to increases in the other which lead to further increases in the first. The multiple positive feedback loops inherent in this model serve to build risk for addictive behaviors over time. More specifically, highly urgent individuals are more likely to consume alcohol which in turn increases their urgent dispositions. This same pattern holds true for individuals with greater expectancies about the reinforcing effects of alcohol. Although not yet demonstrated empirically, change in coping styles may follow a similar pattern, as individuals who engage in emotion-oriented coping tend not to engage in more task-oriented coping responses. As risk builds, this developmental process may become more and more stable in the individual over time.

Further, as this stability builds, the modus operandi may switch from drinking to cope with distress or a negative emotional experience to drinking to avoid the emotional experience altogether. Indeed, well-established substance abuse theory holds that individuals with AD diagnoses are likely to have progressed from alcohol use as a source of negative reinforcement (short-term reduction of distress) to alcohol use as a means of avoiding distress altogether (Baker, Piper, McCarthy, Majeskie, & Fiore, 2004). That is, such individuals learn to drink before they experience subjective distress, thus avoiding the negative affect. Although the focus of this chapter has been on understanding persistence in problem drinking, it is likely that individuals high in urgency, expectancies for reinforcement from drinking, and emotion-oriented coping, are at greatest risk for the development of AD in adulthood.

IMPLICATIONS

Problematic alcohol consumption is associated with a host of negative consequences, such as injury, violence, unintended pregnancy, and alcohol dependence (WHO, 2014; Naimi, Lipscomb, Brewer & Gilbert, 2003). Binge drinking has also come to be seen as a public health problem, as it is associated with health outcomes such as cancer, sexually transmitted infections, chronic disease (i.e., heart disease), and poor pregnancy outcomes (WHO, 2014; Iyasu et al., 2002). In addition, problematic drinking is costly. Losses in workplace productivity, health care expenditures, criminal justice costs, and other expenses as a result of binge drinking were estimated to total $249 billion in the U.S. in 2010 (Sacks, Gonzales, Bouchery, Tomedi, & Brewer, 2010). For these reasons alone, decreases in drinking, perhaps in the form of reducing student likelihood of persistence, are of great importance to U.S. society.

Beyond problematic drinking, the risk factors involved in persistence of problematic alcohol consumption may also serve as markers of other forms of concurrent dysfunction. The above factors are present in the risk process for many maladaptive behaviors. In addition to drinking, urgency predicts bulimic symptoms (Fischer, Peterson, & McCarthy, 2013), drug use (Zapolski, Cyders & Smith, 2009), risky sex (Zapolski et al., 2009), gambling (Cyders & Smith, 2008b), and non-suicidal self-injury (Riley, Combs, Jordan & Smith, 2015). Sensation seeking predicts subsequent risky behavior involvement, risky sexual behavior, and increases in smoking in adults (Doran et al., 2013; Zapolski et al., 2009). Low conscientiousness predicts increased drinking, smoking, and risky sexual behavior in youth (Guller et al., 2015a). Psychosocial expectancies exist for a number of addictive behaviors as well, and have been shown to predict behavior-specific dysfunction, including smoking (Lewis-Esquerre et al., 2005; Guller et al., 2015b), as well as binge eating and purging (Pearson et al.,

2012, Pearson & Smith, 2015; Smith et al., 2007). Further, individuals with these outcomes are likely to face problems in their occupational lives and interpersonal relationships. As such, persistence in problematic drinking may represent just one facet of a larger developmental difficulty – problematic adjustment to adulthood (Settles & Smith, 2015). For these reasons, it is important to consider these risk factors as targets for assessment prevention and intervention efforts.

In considering the implications of this theory for prevention and intervention methods, we first discuss the importance of identifying individuals with high-risk personality traits and high-risk expectancies. Following this, we consider treatments based on high-risk personality traits. We then review efforts regarding expectancy-based treatment and skills based coping methods.

Identification of College Students at Risk to Persist

As argued above, the widespread culture of drinking on college campuses blurs differences between those students who will successfully transition into early adulthood and those who may not, as their drinking behaviors may look largely the same. Those at risk for adult persistence and those not may well appear indistinguishable based on diagnostic status, or even drinking behavior alone. Therefore, these at-risk individuals must be identified by different metrics. As suggested by the model we have presented, evaluating students on their levels of urgency and sensation seeking, their alcohol expectancies, and their coping styles has the potential to be efficacious in clarifying risk status. There are both questionnaire and interview measures to assess the urgency traits, as well as to assess sensation seeking, lack of planning, and lack of perseverance (the measure is called the UPPS-P and is available from the authors: Lynam, Smith, Cyders, Fischer, & Whiteside, 2007). With respect to alcohol, Smith and Goldman (1994) provided cutting scores, i.e., scores on the measure of the expectancy that alcohol can enhance or impede social behavior (from the AEQ-A:

Christiansen, Goldman, & Inn, 1982), that identify youth at particular risk to begin drinking over the following 24 months. Their work was on adolescents; more needs to be done to identify emerging adult cutting scores to predict persistence into adulthood. Several coping metrics exist in the literature including the Coping Inventory for Stressful Situations (CISS; Ender & Parker, 1990), the COPE (Carver et al., 1989, and the Ways of Coping checklist (WOC; Folkman & Lazarus, 1985). The development and utilization of cut scores for impulsigenic traits, specifically urgency, alcohol expectancies, and for maladaptive coping styles would be a viable and important avenue of research.

Prevention and Intervention Efforts

There is a wealth of evidence to suggest that problematic drinking begins far before the college years for a large portion of youth. Chung et al. (2012) found that alcohol consumption rates increase from 7-10% in late childhood to 40-50% by the end of the first year of high school. Therefore, many prevention efforts may have greatest impact before or during early adolescence. The development of school-based prevention strategies that target transdiagnostic risk stemming from impulsive personality traits and behavior-specific risk from learned expectancies would be a useful avenue of applied research. Such strategies may also find it useful to address coping styles by encouraging the development of adaptive coping strategies well before the collegiate and young adult years.

Regarding intervention efforts, the utilization of Dialectical Behavior Therapy (DBT: Linehan, 1993) techniques for individuals high in negative urgency has been suggested due to the trait's overlap with many behaviors common to borderline personality disorder (Zapolski, Settles, Cyders, & Smith, 2010). DBT emphasizes four categories of skills - distress tolerance, interpersonal effectiveness, emotion regulation, and mindfulness - that are designed to manage distress and prevent rash action (Linehan, 1993). Goals of DBT involve increased toleration of distress and intense emotions without engaging in immediate action, effective communication of emotional experience to others, and adjustment of emotional reactions by considering the context, as well as learning to identify precipitating events or triggers to emotional reactivity. While the primary purpose of treatments like DBT has not been to alter personality traits such as negative urgency, but rather the goals listed above, personality change may occur as a result of these treatments. One study of African American women with PTSD has shown that negative urgency was reduced following a one-hour emotion regulation training (Weiss et al., 2015). As such, these strategies may be effective in collegiate populations.

Regarding psychosocial learning intervention, there is evidence that expectancies can be challenged and manipulated experimentally. A recent meta-analysis of alcohol expectancy challenge interventions with college students by Scott-Sheldon, Terry, Carey, Garey, and Carey (2012) revealed that participants exposed to expectancy challenges reported lower positive alcohol expectancies, reduced alcohol use, and reduced frequency of heavy drinking. These effects operated within individuals exposed to expectancy challenges and they were not present in members of control groups. However, these effects were not maintained at follow-ups greater than 4 weeks. Among the possible conclusions from this review are these: (1) perhaps the specific nature of the expectancy challenge is important; (2) perhaps intervening earlier than the college years would be more effective; and (3) lasting interventions may well need to target multiple risk factors, not just expectancies.

More broadly, addressing multiple components of the risk model described above may prove important. In the field of eating disorders, researchers have developed such a treatment, called Integrative Cognitive-Affective Therapy for Bulimia Nervosa (ICAT-BN: Wonderlich et al., 2014). ICAT-BN includes interventions that target negative urgency, cognitive risk factors such as expectancies, and introduces alternative means of coping. Early tests of the intervention are promising (Accurso et al., 2016; Wonderlich et al., 2014), and it may serve as a useful starting point for a similar alcohol-based intervention.

CONCLUSION

We have presented an overview of a model of risk for persistence of problematic alcohol use following the collegiate years into young adulthood. This model may prove promising in the differentiation of students who persist in their problematic patterns of drinking into young adulthood and those who do not at a time when their drinking behavior cannot be easily distinguished. Impulsigenic personality traits, such as urgency, expectancies regarding the reinforcing effects of drinking, such as social facilitation and negative affect reduction, and maladaptive coping styles, such as emotion-oriented coping, have all been implicated in the development of problematic drinking behavior. As such, each is likely to confer risk for persistent and problematic alcohol use. Further, the transaction between these risk factors is likely to enhance such risks.

It is important to appreciate that the model we have presented addresses one set of factors likely to increase risk for problem drinking persistence: individual difference factors. Ultimately, transactions among individual difference factors and environmental/contextual factors are likely to best account for risk. Contrast young adults without employment or committed relationships to those with both. In the former case, there are fewer environmental disincentives for heavy drinking, so perhaps only moderate levels of individual difference risk are necessary to lead to problem drinking. In the latter case, there are clear reasons to avoid heavy drinking, so perhaps higher levels of individual difference risk need to be present before problem drinking is likely.

There may be other transactional processes between individual difference and environment-based risk. If high levels of urgency and problem drinking reflect more pervasive developmental adjustment difficulties (Settles & Smith, 2015), it may be the case that individuals elevated on these individual difference risk factors are likely also to be elevated in environmental risk. This could occur if individual problem behavior reduces the likelihood of successful employment and relationships (Roberts, Walton, Bogg, & Caspi, 2006). Research into the possibility of transactional, negative feedback loops between individual difference and environmental risk processes may well prove important.

Empirical tests of the individual difference model we have presented, and further development of broader integrative models, are of great importance and will likely inform intervention and prevention efforts. Other next steps include the development of cut scores for established measures of these variables, the implementation and evaluation of early prevention efforts in childhood and adolescence, and the development of intervention efforts that target each component of risk. These tasks are vital in the reduction of risk for an unsuccessful transition into emerging adulthood.

REFERENCES

Accurso, E. C., Wonderlich, S. A., Crosby, R. D., Smith, T. L., Klein, M. H., Mitchell, J. E., ... & Peterson, C. B. (2016). Predictors and moderators of treatment outcome in a randomized clinical trial for adults with symptoms of bulimia nervosa. *Journal of Consulting and Clinical Psychology*, *84*(2), 178-184.

Ajzen, I., & Fishbein, M. (1980). *Understanding attitudes and predicting social behaviour.* Pearson.

Bachman, J. G., Johnston, L. D., & O'Malley, P. M. (1981). Smoking, drinking, and drug use among American high school students: correlates and trends, 1975-1979. *American Journal of Public Health*, *71*(1), 59-69.

Bachman, J. G., O'Malley, P. M., & Johnston, L. D. (1984). Drug use among young adults: the impacts of role status and social environment. *Journal of personality and social psychology*, *47*(3), 629-645.

Baker, T. B., Piper, M. E., McCarthy, D. E., Majeskie, M. R., & Fiore, M. C. (2004). Addiction motivation reformulated: An affective processing model of negative reinforcement. *Psychological Review, 111*, 33-51.

Berg, J. M., Latzman, R. D., Bliwise, N. G., & Lilienfeld, S. O. (2015). Parsing the heterogeneity of impulsivity: A meta-analytic review of the behavioral implications of the UPPS for psychopathology. *Psychological Assessment*, *27*(4), 1129-1146.

Birkley, E. L., & Smith, G. T. (2011). Recent advances in understanding the personality underpinnings of impulsive behavior and their role in risk for addictive behaviors. *Current Drug Abuse Reviews*, *4*(4), 215-227.

Bolles, R. C. (1972). Reinforcement, expectancy, and learning. *Psychological Review*, *79*(5), 394-409.

Brandon, T. H., & Baker, T. B. (1991). The Smoking Consequences Questionnaire: The subjective expected utility of smoking in college students. *Psychological Assessment: A Journal of Consulting and Clinical Psychology*, *3*(3), 484-491.

Bruder-Mattson, S. F., & Hovanitz, C. A. (1990). Coping and attributional styles as predictors of depression. *Journal of Clinical Psychology*, *46*(5), 557-565.

Carver, C. S., Scheier, M. F., & Weintraub, J. K. (1989). Assessing coping strategies: a theoretically based approach. *Journal of Personality and Social Psychology*, *56*(2), 267-283.

Christiansen, B. A., Goldman, M. S., & Inn, A. (1982). Development of alcohol-related expectancies in adolescents: Separating pharmacological from social-learning influences. *Journal of Consulting and Clinical Psychology*, *50*(3), 336-344.

Chung, T., Smith, G. T., Donovan, J. E., Windle, M., Faden, V. B., Chen, C. M., & Martin, C. S. (2012). Drinking frequency as a brief screen for adolescent alcohol problems. *Pediatrics, 129*, 205–212.

Cole, H. A., Peterson, S. J., & Smith, G. T. (2018) *Biological, behavioral, and personality predictors of adolescents' preferred style of coping.* Manuscript submitted for publication.

Compas, B. E., Connor-Smith, J. K., Saltzman, H., Thomsen, A. H., & Wadsworth, M. E. (2001). Coping with stress during childhood and adolescence: problems, progress, and potential in theory and research. *Psychological Bulletin, 127*(1), 87-127.

Compas, B. E., Malcarne, V. L., & Fondacaro, K. M. (1988). Coping with stressful events in older children and young adolescents. *Journal of Consulting and Clinical Psychology*, *56*(3), 405-411.

Corbin, W. R., Iwamoto, D. K., & Fromme, K. (2011). A comprehensive longitudinal test of the acquired preparedness model for alcohol use and related problems. *Journal of Studies on Alcohol and Drugs*, *72*(4), 602-610.

Coskunpinar, A., Dir, A. L., & Cyders, M. A. (2013). Multidimensionality in impulsivity and alcohol Use: a meta-analysis using the UPPS model of impulsivity. *Alcoholism: Clinical and Experimental Research*, *37*(9), 1441-1450.

Costa, P. T, Jr., & McCrae, R. R. (1992). Normal personality assessment in clinical practice: The NEO Personality Inventory. *Psychological Assessment, 4*, 5-13.

Cyders, M. A., Flory, K., Rainer, S., & Smith, G. T. (2009). The role of personality dispositions to risky behavior in predicting first-year college drinking. *Addiction*, *104*(2), 193-202.

Cyders, M. A., & Smith, G. T. (2007). Mood-based rash action and its components: Positive and negative urgency. *Personality and Individual Differences, 43(4),* 839-850.

Cyders, M. A., & Smith, G. T. (2008a). Emotion-based dispositions to rash action: Positive and negative urgency. *Psychological Bulletin, 134(6),* 807-828.

Cyders, M. A., & Smith, G. T. (2008b). Clarifying the role of personality dispositions in risk for increased gambling behavior. *Personality and Individual Differences, 45*(6), 503-508.

Cyders, M. A., Zapolski, T. C., Combs, J. L., Settles, R. F., Fillmore, M. T., & Smith, G. T. (2010). Experimental effect of positive urgency on negative outcomes from risk taking and on increased alcohol consumption. *Psychology of Addictive Behaviors*, *24*(3), 367-375.

Darkes, J., & Goldman, M. S. (1993). Expectancy challenge and drinking reduction: Experimental evidence for a mediational process. *Journal of Consulting and Clinical Psychology, 61*(2), 344-353.

Davis, H. A., Riley, E. N., & Smith, G. T. (in press). Transactions among personality and psychosocial learning risk factors for adolescent drinking: The acquired preparedness model of risk. In P. M. Monti, S. M. Colby, and T. A. O'Leary (Eds.). *Adolescents, Alcohol, and*

Substance Abuse: Reaching Teens through Brief Interventions, 2nd edition. New York: Guilford Press.

Doran, N., Khoddam, R., Sanders, P. E., Schweizer, C. A., Trim, R. S., & Myers, M. G. (2013). A prospective study of the acquired preparedness model: The effects of impulsivity and expectancies on smoking initiation in college students. *Psychology of Addictive Behaviors*, *27*(3), 714-722.

Dubow, E. F., & Tisak, J. (1989). The relation between stressful life events and adjustment in elementary school children: The role of social support and social problem-solving skills. *Child Development*, 1412-1423.

Dubow, E. F., Tisak, J., Causey, D., Hryshko, A., & Reid, G. (1991). A two-year longitudinal study of stressful life events, social support, and social problem-solving skills: Contributions to children's behavioral and academic adjustment. *Child Development*, *62*(3), 583-599.

Edwards, M. J., & Holden, R. R. (2001). Coping, meaning in life, and suicidal manifestations: Examining gender differences. *Journal of Clinical Psychology*, *57*(12), 1517-1534.

Endler, N. S., & Parker, J. D. A. (1999) *Coping Inventory for Stressful Situations (CISS): Manual (Revised Edition)*, Multi-Health Systems, Inc., Toronto.

Ellickson, P. L., Tucker, J. S., & Klein, D. J. (2003). Ten-year prospective study of public health problems associated with early drinking. *Pediatrics, 111*(5), 949-955.

Fischer, S., Smith, G. T., & Cyders, M. A. (2008). Another look at impulsivity: A meta-analytic review comparing specific dispositions to rash action in their relationship to bulimic symptoms. *Clinical Psychology Review*, *28*(8), 1413-1425.

Fischer, S., Peterson, C. M., & McCarthy, D. (2013). A prospective test of the influence of negative urgency and expectancies on binge eating and purging. *Psychology of Addictive Behaviors, 27*(1), 294–300.

Folkman, S., & Lazarus, R. S. (1985). If it changes it must be a process: study of emotion and coping during three stages of a college examination. *Journal of Personality and Social Psychology*, *48*(1), 150-170.

Gates, J. R., Corbin, W. R., & Fromme, K. (2016). Emerging adult identity development, alcohol use, and alcohol-related problems during the transition out of college. *Psychology of Addictive Behaviors*, *30*(3), 345-355.

Glyshaw, K., Cohen, L. H., & Towbes, L. C. (1989). Coping strategies and psychological distress: Prospective analyses of early and middle adolescents. *American Journal of Community Psychology*, *17*(5), 607-623.

Goldberg, J. H., Halpern-Felsher, B. L., & Millstein, S. G. (2002). Beyond invulnerability: the importance of benefits in adolescents' decision to drink alcohol. *Health Psychology*, *21*(5), 477-484.

Goldman, M. S., Brown, S. A., Christiansen, B. A., & Smith, G. T. (1991). Alcoholism and memory: Broadening the scope of alcohol-expectancy research. *Psychological Bulletin, 110*(1), 137-146.

Goldman, M. S., Darkes, J., & Del Boca, F. K. (1999). Expectancy mediation of biopsychosocial risk for alcohol use and alcoholism. *Experimental and Clinical Psychopharmacology, 12*(1), 27-38.

Goldman, M. S., Reich, R. R., & Darkes, J. (2006). Expectancy as a unifying construct in alcohol-related cognition. *Handbook of Implicit Cognition and Addiction*, 105-119.

Gotham, H. J., Sher, K. J., & Wood, P. K. (1997). Predicting stability and change in frequency of intoxication from the college years to beyond: Individual-difference and role transition variables. *Journal of Abnormal Psychology*, *106*(4), 619.

Guller, L., Zapolski, T. C., & Smith, G. T. (2015a). Personality measured in elementary school predicts middle school addictive behavior involvement. *Journal of Psychopathology and Behavioral Assessment, 37*(3), 523-532.

Guller, L., Zapolski, T. C. B., & Smith, G. T. (2015b). Longitudinal test of a reciprocal model of smoking expectancies and smoking experience in youth. *Psychology of Addictive Behaviors, 29*(1), 201-210.

Gunn, R. L., & Smith, G. T. (2010). Risk factors for elementary school drinking: Pubertal status, personality, and alcohol expectancies concurrently predict fifth grade alcohol consumption. *Psychology of Addictive Behaviors*, *24*(4), 617-627.

Hedden, S. L. (2015). *Behavioral health trends in the United States: results from the 2014 National Survey on Drug Use and Health.* Substance Abuse and Mental Health Services Administration, Department of Health & Human Services.

Hingson, R., Heeren, T., Winter, M., & Wechsler, H. (2005). Magnitude of alcohol-related mortality and morbidity among US college students ages 18–24: Changes from 1998 to 2001. *Annual Review of Public Health*, *26*, 259-279.

Hingson, R. W., Zha, W., & Weitzman, E. R. (2009). Magnitude of and trends in alcohol-related mortality and morbidity among US college students ages 18-24, 1998-2005. *Journal of Studies on Alcohol and Drugs, Supplement*, (16), 12-20.

Iyasu, S., Randall, L. L., Welty, T. K., Hsia, J., Kinney, H. C., Mandell, F., ... & Willinger, M. (2002). Risk factors for sudden infant death syndrome among northern plains Indians. *Journal of the American Medical Association*, *288*(21), 2717-2723.

Jackson, K. M., & Sher, K. J. (2005). Similarities and differences of longitudinal phenotypes across alternate indices of alcohol involvement: a methodologic comparison of trajectory approaches. *Psychology of Addictive Behaviors*, *19*(4), 339-351.

Jackson, K. M., Sher, K. J., Gotham, H. J., & Wood, P. K. (2001). Transitioning into and out of large-effect drinking in young adulthood. *Journal of Abnormal Psychology*, *110*(3), 378-391.

Jochman, K. A., & Fromme, K. (2010). Maturing out of substance use: The other side of etiology. In L. Scheier (Ed.), *Handbook of drug use etiology: Theory, methods, and empirical findings* (pp. 565-578). Washington, DC, US: American Psychological Association.

Kaiser, A. J., Davis, H. A., Milich, R., Smith, G. T., and Charnigo, R. (in press). Bidirectional relations of impulsive personality and alcohol use. *Substance Use and Misuse.*

Koff, E., & Sangani, P. (1997). Effects of coping style and negative body image on eating disturbance. *International Journal of Eating Disorders, 22*(1), 51-56.

Lau-Barraco, C., & Dunn, M. E. (2008). Evaluation of a single-session expectancy challenge intervention to reduce alcohol use among college students. *Psychology of Addictive Behaviors, 22*(2), 168-175.

Lewis-Esquerre, J. M., Rodrigue, J. R., & Kahler, C. W. (2005). Development and validation of an adolescent smoking consequences questionnaire. *Nicotine & Tobacco Research, 7*(1), 81-90.

Linehan, M. M. (1993). Dialectical behavior therapy for treatment of borderline personality disorder: implications for the treatment of substance abuse. *NIDA research monograph, 137*, 201-216.

Littlefield, A. K., Sher, K. J., & Wood, P. K. (2009). Is "maturing out" of problematic alcohol involvement related to personality change? *Journal of Abnormal Psychology, 118*(2), 360-374.

Littlefield, A. K., Vergés, A., Rosinski, J. M., Steinley, D., & Sher, K. J. (2013). Motivational typologies of drinkers: Do enhancement and coping drinkers form two distinct groups? *Addiction, 108*(3), 497-503.

Loumidis, K., & Wells, A. (2001). Exercising for the wrong reasons: Relationships among eating disorder beliefs, dysfunctional exercise beliefs and coping. *Clinical Psychology & Psychotherapy, 8*(6), 416-423.

Lynam, D., Smith, G. T., Cyders, M. A., Fischer, S., & Whiteside, S. A. (2007). *The UPPS-P: A multidimensional measure of risk for impulsive behavior.* Unpublished technical report.

Miller, P. M., Smith, G. T., & Goldman, M. S. (1990). Emergence of alcohol expectancies in childhood: A possible critical period. *Journal of Studies on Alcohol and Drugs, 51*(4), 343-349.

Naimi, T. S., Lipscomb, L. E., Brewer, R. D., & Gilbert, B. C. (2003). Binge drinking in the preconception period and the risk of unintended pregnancy: implications for women and their children. *Pediatrics, 111*(Supplement 1), 1136-1141.

Ouellette, J. A., Gerrard, M., Gibbons, F. X., & Reis-Bergan, M. (1999). Parents, peers, and prototypes: Antecedents of adolescent alcohol expectancies, alcohol consumption, and alcohol-related life problems in rural youth. *Psychology of Addictive Behaviors, 13*(3), 183-197.

Pearson, C. M., Combs, J. L., Zapolski, T. C., & Smith, G. T. (2012). A longitudinal transactional risk model for early eating disorder onset. *Journal of Abnormal Psychology, 121*(3), 707-718.

Pearson, C. M., & Smith, G. T. (2015). Bulimic symptom onset in young girls: A longitudinal trajectory analysis. *Journal of Abnormal Psychology, 124*(4), 1003–1013.

Peterson, S. J., Davis, H. A. & Smith, G. T. (in press) Personality and learning predictors of adolescent alcohol consumption trajectories. *Journal of Abnormal Psychology.*

Peterson, S. J. & Smith, G. T. (2016). Application of the expectancy concept to substance use. Invited chapter in S. A. Brown and R. A. Zucker (Eds.), *Oxford Handbook of Adolescent Substance Abuse*. DOI: 10.1093/oxfordhb/9780199735662.013.017

Peterson, S. J. & Smith, G. T. (2017). Association between elementary school personality and high school smoking and drinking. *Addiction. 112*(11), 2043-2052.

Rafnsson, F. D., Jonsson, F. H., & Windle, M. (2006). Coping strategies, stressful life events, problem behaviors, and depressed affect. *Anxiety, stress, and Coping, 19*(3), 241-257.

Riley, E. N. Combs, J. L., Jordan, C. E., & Smith, G. T. (2015). Negative urgency and lack of perseverance: Identification of differential pathways of onset and maintenance risk in the longitudinal prediction of non-suicidal self-injury. *Behavior Therapy, 46*, 439–448.

Riley, E. N., Rukavina, M., & Smith, G. T. (2016). The reciprocal predictive relationship between high-risk personality and drinking: An 8-wave longitudinal study in early adolescents. *Journal of Abnormal Psychology, 125*(6), 798-804.

Roberts, B. W., Walton, K., Bogg, T., & Caspi, A. (2006). De-investment in work and non-normative personality trait change in young adulthood. *European Journal of Personality, 20*(6), 461-474.

Rotter, J. B. (1975). Some problems and misconceptions related to the construct of internal versus external control of reinforcement. *Journal of Consulting and Clinical Psychology*, *43*(1), 56-67.

Rutledge, P. C., & Sher, K. J. (2001). Heavy drinking from the freshman year into early young adulthood: the roles of stress, tension-reduction drinking motives, gender and personality. *Journal of Studies on Alcohol*, *62*(4), 457-466.

Sacks, J. J., Gonzales, K. R., Bouchery, E. E., Tomedi, L. E., & Brewer, R. D. (2015). 2010 national and state costs of excessive alcohol consumption. *American Journal of Preventive Medicine*, *49*(5), e73-e79.

Scott-Sheldon, L. A., Terry, D. L., Carey, K. B., Garey, L., & Carey, M. P. (2012). Efficacy of expectancy challenge interventions to reduce college student drinking: A meta-analytic review. *Psychology of Addictive Behaviors*, *26*(3), 393-405.

Settles, R. F., Cyders, M., & Smith, G. T. (2010). Longitudinal validation of the acquired preparedness model of drinking risk. *Psychology of Addictive Behaviors*, *24*(2), 198-208.

Settles, R. E., Zapolski, T. C., & Smith, G. T. (2014). Longitudinal test of a developmental model of the transition to early drinking. *Journal of Abnormal Psychology*, *123*(1), 141-151.

Settles, R. E., & Smith, G. T. (2015). Toward a developmentally centered approach to adolescent alcohol and substance use treatment. *Current Drug Abuse Reviews, 8*, 134-151.

Sher, K. J., & Trull, T. J. (1994). Personality and disinhibitory psychopathology: alcoholism and antisocial personality disorder. *Journal of Abnormal Psychology*, *103*(1), 92-102.

Sher, K. J., Bartholow, B. D., & Nanda, S. (2001). Short-and long-term effects of fraternity and sorority membership on heavy drinking: a social norms perspective. *Psychology of Addictive Behaviors*, *15*(1), 42-51.

Slutske, W. S. (2005). Alcohol use disorders among US college students and their non–college-attending peers. *Archives of General Psychiatry*, *62*(3), 321-327.

Smith, G. T., & Goldman, M. S. (1994). Alcohol expectancy theory and the identification of high-risk adolescents. *Journal of Research on Adolescence*, *4*(2), 229-247.

Smith, G. T., Goldman, M. S., Greenbaum, P. E., & Christiansen, B. A. (1995). Expectancy for social facilitation from drinking: the divergent paths of high-expectancy and low-expectancy adolescents. *Journal of Abnormal Psychology, 104*(1), 32-40.

Smith, G. T., Simmons, J. R., Flory, K., Annus, A. M., & Hill, K. K. (2007). Thinness and eating expectancies predict subsequent binge eating and purging behavior among adolescent girls. *Journal of Abnormal Psychology, 116*, 188–197.

Smith, G. T., Williams, S. Fister, Cyders, M., & Kelley, S. (2006). Reactive personality-environment transactions and adult developmental trajectories. *Developmental Psychology, 42,* 877-887.

Spoor, S. T., Bekker, M. H., Van Strien, T., & van Heck, G. L. (2007). Relations between negative affect, coping, and emotional eating. *Appetite, 48(3),* 368-376.

Stautz, K., & Cooper, A. (2013). Impulsivity-related personality traits and adolescent alcohol use: a meta-analytic review. *Clinical Psychology Review*, *33*(4), 574-592.

Tolman, E. C. (1932). *Purposive Behavior in Animals and Men.* University of California Press.

Tucker, J. S., Orlando, M., & Ellickson, P. L. (2003). Patterns and correlates of binge drinking trajectories from early adolescence to young adulthood. *Health Psychology, 22*(1), 79-87.

Vergés, A., Jackson, K. M., Bucholz, K. K., Grant, J. D., Trull, T. J., Wood, P. K., & Sher, K. J. (2012). Deconstructing the age-prevalence curve of alcohol dependence: Why "maturing out" is only a small piece of the puzzle. *Journal of Abnormal Psychology*, *121*(2), 511-23.

Wardell, J. D., Read, J. P., Colder, C. R., & Merrill, J. E. (2012). Positive alcohol expectancies mediate the influence of the behavioral activation system on alcohol use: A prospective path analysis. *Addictive Behaviors*, *37*(4), 435-443.

Weiss, N. H., Tull, M. T., Davis, L. T., Searcy, J., Williams, I., & Gratz, K. L. (2015). A Preliminary Experimental Investigation of Emotion Dysregulation and Impulsivity in Risky Behaviours. *Behaviour Change, 32*(02), 127-142.

Whiteside, S. P., & Lynam, D. R. (2001). The five factor model and impulsivity: Using a structural model of personality to understand impulsivity. *Personality and Individual Differences, 30(4),* 669-689.

WHO Management of Substance Abuse Unit. (2014). *Global status report on alcohol and health, 2014.* World Health Organization.

Wills, T. A., Sandy, J. M., Yaeger, A. M., Cleary, S. D., & Shinar, O. (2001). Coping dimensions, life stress, and adolescent substance use: A latent growth analysis. *Journal of Abnormal Psychology, 110(2),* 309-323.

Windle, M., & Windle, R. C. (1996). Coping strategies, drinking motives, and stressful life events among middle adolescents: Associations with emotional and behavioral problems and with academic functioning. *Journal of Abnormal Psychology*, *105*(4), 551-560.

Wonderlich, S. A., Peterson, C. B., Crosby, R. D., Smith, T. L., Klein, M. H., Mitchell, J. E., & Crow, S. J. (2014). A randomized controlled comparison of integrative cognitive-affective therapy (ICAT) and enhanced cognitive-behavioral therapy (CBT-E) for bulimia nervosa. *Psychological Medicine*, *44*(03), 543-553.

Zapolski, T. C., Cyders, M. A., & Smith, G. T. (2009). Positive urgency predicts illegal drug use and risky sexual behavior. *Psychology of Addictive Behaviors, 23*(2), 348–354.

Zapolski, T. C., Settles, R. E., Cyders, M. A., & Smith, G. T. (2010). Borderline personality disorder, bulimia nervosa, antisocial personality disorder, ADHD, substance use: common threads, common treatment needs, and the nature of impulsivity. *Independent Practitioner (Lutterworth, England)*, *30*(1), 20-23.

Zucker, R. A. (1986). The four alcoholisms: a developmental account of the etiologic process. In *Nebraska symposium on motivation*. University of Nebraska Press.

Zucker, R. A. (1994). Pathways to alcohol problems and alcoholism: A developmental account of the evidence for multiple alcoholisms and for contextual contributions to risk. (In R. A. Zucker, J. Howard, & G. Boyd (Eds.), *The development of alcohol problems: Exploring the biopsychosocial matrix of risk* (pp. 255-289). Rockville, MD: National Institute on Alcohol Abuse and Alcoholism.

Zucker, R. A., Kincaid, S. B., Fitzgerald, H. E., & Bingham, C. R. (1995). Alcohol schema acquisition in preschoolers: Differences between children of alcoholics and children of nonalcoholics. *Alcoholism: Clinical and Experimental Research, 19*(4), 1011-1017.

In: Understanding Impulsive Behavior
Editor: Christian Braddon
ISBN: 978-1-53613-815-3

Chapter 3

RELEVANT TOPICS FOR UNDERSTANDING IMPULSIVE BEHAVIORS IN ADOLESCENCE

***Alice Rodrigues Willhelm*[1], *PhD*,**
***Anderson Siqueira Pereira*[1], *PhD*,**
Paula Madeira Fortes*[1], *PhD
and Rosa Maria Martins de Almeida*[2], *PhD
Federal University of Rio Grande do Sul (UFRGS),
Porto Alegre, Brazil

ABSTRACT

Adolescence is a period of life in which individuals pass through several changes, including experiencing new situations and new relationships with peers, parents, and superiors. This phase of life is also marked by physical and brain development. The last area to develop in the central nervous system is the prefrontal cortex (PFC), which is also linked to the ability to control impulses. This suggests that adolescents tend to have more impulsive behaviors than adults that can result in risky behaviors such as alcohol and drugs. This impulsivity can be characterized by cognitive and behavioral patterns which may lead to short- and long-term consequences. This impulsivity can be divided into three different dimensions: motor, attentional, and non-planning. Besides the discussion about impulsivity in adolescence, which may be associated with risk behaviors such as drug use, the socioeconomic status is relevant in this discussion as well, because studies found differences between socioeconomic status and executive functions in adolescents and preadolescents. Lower inhibitory control and lower performance in executive functions were related to childhood poverty. In addition, brain development occurs differently between boys and girls, which may result in differences in impulsivity between genders. So, the purpose of this chapter is to discuss impulsivity in adolescence and clarify issues that may help understand topics related to this, such as the difference in impulsive behaviors between genders at this stage of life and what influence socioeconomic status may have on such behaviors.

1. Adolescence and Impulsive Behavior

Preadolescence and adolescence are characterized by biological, physiological, and behavioral changes. Those periods of life occur between ages 10 and 19 (Casey, Jones, & Hare, 2008; Dahl & Gunnar, 2009). This period of transition to adulthood begins at puberty, in which individuals experience physical and cerebral maturation, hormonal revolution, increased social interaction, increased responsibilities, and experience new situations (Shirtcliff, Dahl, & Pollak, 2009).

Those periods of life are also marked by risk behavior and impulsivity, in which there are difficulties in inhibitory control (Crone, 2009; Shirtcliff et al., 2009). Impulsive behaviors are frequently associated in adolescence with alcohol and drug use, unprotected sex and outlaw activities (Casey & Jones, 2010; Verdejo-García, Lawrence, & Clark, 2008).

Studies suggest that impulsive and risky behaviors may be associated with brain maturation, which is not yet complete at this stage of life (Mills, Goddings, Clasen, Giedd, & Blakemore, 2014; Romer, Reyna, & Satterthwaite, 2017). Studies suggest that the brain region of the prefrontal cortex is critical for controlling attention, reasoning, and behavior, and it is the last to develop, fully maturing only in late adolescence or early adulthood (Adleman et al., 2002; Aron, Fletcher, Bullmore, Sahakian, & Robbins,

2003; Crone, 2009; Luna, Garver, Urban, Lazar, & Sweeney, 2004; Sowell, Thompson, Tessner, & Toga, 2001).

These issues are also directly related to the executive functions that are processes that support several daily activities, such as flexibility of reasoning, concentrated attention, inhibitory planning and control (Barros & Hazin, 2013; Best, Miller, & Jones, 2009; Corso, Sperb, de Jou, & Salles, 2013; Luna et al., 2004). Some studies indicate that younger children have a lower level of activity in the prefrontal cortex while performing tasks of executive functions, when compared with older children, which suggests that as this region develops, an improvement occurs in these functions (Adleman et al., 2002; Luna et al., 2004).

The same can be observed with regard to impulsivity, there is decrease of impulsivity through adolescence. Preadolescents from ages 11 to 13 show higher levels of impulsivity than those adolescents who are 16 years old (Niv, Tuvblad, Raine, Wang, & Baker, 2012). The impulsivity can be characterized for cognitive and behavior patterns which may lead to short-long term consequences and occur when there is a thoughtless and unplanned change in the individual's action (Malloy-Diniz et al., 2010; Moeller, Barratt, Dougherty, Schmitz, & Swann, 2001). Besides, the impulsivity can be divided in three different dimensions: motor impulsiveness, related to a deficit in response inhibition; attentional impulsiveness, related to a difficulty to resist tempting stimuli; and non-planning impulsiveness, related to inability to make a long-term planning (Malloy-Diniz et al., 2010). The decrease of these characteristics, with the increase of inhibitory control, occurs by a maturity in brain system (especially prefrontal cortex) through adolescence (Hare et al., 2008).

However, during adolescence, inhibitory control is still maturing and impulsive behaviors appear more frequently, and, along with them, risk behaviors emerge. In this phase, adolescents try alcohol and drugs and these are the classic risk behaviors of adolescence (Botvin & Griffin, 2007). International studies have presented worrisome results regarding alcohol consumption in adolescence, since there is a high consumption of alcoholic beverages at this stage of life (Asbridge, Cartwright, Wilson, & Langille, 2016; Botvin & Griffin, 2007; Carvalho Malta, Medeiros Mascarenhas,

Lopes Porto, Barreto, & de Morais Neto, 2014; de Almeida et al., 2014; Willhelm et al., 2015).

An important issue to be highlighted is that when ingested, alcoholic beverages have a depressant effect on the central nervous system, reducing the effectiveness of executive functions (Domingues, Mendonça, Laranjeira, & Nakamura-Palacios, 2009). High impulsivity scores are also associated with alcohol consumption. Some studies suggest that the presence of impulsivity may lead to the experimentation or use of early alcohol, as well as other risk behaviors (Casey & Jones, 2010; Spear, 2013). However, a meta-analytical review on the topic suggested that the link between impulsivity and alcohol consumption is perhaps best seen as a reciprocal process in which high levels of impulsive behavior influence the increase in alcohol consumption and are even more exacerbated due to neurobiological changes caused by alcohol (Stautz & Cooper, 2013).

Another study with adolescents (n = 534) suggested that weakness in executive functions may predict the onset of alcohol use in adolescence (Peeters et al., 2015). Results from the same study also pointed that low scores in working memory were able to predict the habit of binge drinking in the sample (Peeters et al., 2015). However, it still pointed out that the continuous and heavy use of alcohol can weaken and/or further increase these weaknesses in executive functions, intensifying impulsive behaviors.

2. Socioeconomic Status, Environment and Impulsive Behavior

As mentioned before, impulsive behavior can be a risk factor for several harmful behaviors to the development of young people; however, it must be clear that, in addition to this risk factor, the environment in which the young person is inserted plays an important role. Increasingly, studies demonstrate the importance of the interaction of biological or genetic factors and the environment.

Studies discuss differences between socioeconomic status (SES) and executive functions in adolescents and preadolescents in which lower inhibitory control and lower performance in executive functions were found in relation to socioeconomic status, linked do childhood poverty (Hackman & Farah, 2009; Sarsour et al., 2011). Another study found higher total and non-planning impulsivity and less inhibitory control in low SES students compared to medium and high SES (Willhelm, Viacava, Cabral, VanMeter, & de Almeida, in press).

Young people at a disadvantage and poverty often deal with adversity and this chronic exposure to environmental stressors can have negative and lasting effects on health and well-being, being related to a higher prevalence of emotional, mental or behavioral disorders and lower resilience (Bethell, Gombojav, Solloway, & Wissow, 2016). These situations can lead to emotional and social trauma and include situations such as physical, emotional, or sexual abuse, serious economic difficulties, witnessing or experiencing violence at home or in the neighborhood, problems with alcohol and substance use by parents, parental divorce, and loss of parents or legal guardians to death or incarceration (Bethell et al., 2016; Sacks, Murphey, & Moore, 2014). Therefore, high exposure to these situations is strongly associated with the consequences on the mental health of children and adults (Beesdo-Baum & Knappe, 2012; Beesdo, Knappe, & Pine, 2009; Giovanelli, Reynolds, Mondi, & Ou, 2016; Turner et al., 2016).

Chronic exposure to these stressors affects the development of the brain systems involved in these processes, which can lead to physiological and behavioral changes. Adolescents are already more susceptible due to incomplete brain maturation, and these situations can have negative impact in the development of inhibitory control, resulting in less self-control and use of maladaptive strategies. Studies already relate the greater exposure to stress with greater risk of developing addictive behaviors, such as substance use (Sinha, 2008). Therefore, exposure to stress increases vulnerability to risky behavior. In addition, many risk behaviors are observed more frequently in the neighborhood and even within the home, modeling and encouraging a repertoire of unhealthy strategies such as substance use and violence.

During adolescence, there are three important contexts that greatly influence the behaviors of the young: the family, the school, and the peer group. Each context has a different weight, but all influence the behaviors of the young, being able to act as factors of protection, as well as risk factors. Moreover, research indicates that the socioeconomic level in which these contexts are inserted influences their positive or negative character.

The family tends to play an important role in the life of the children throughout the life cycle (Ginsburg, 2007). During adolescence, it has the role of helping young people deal with issues related to their impulses, as well as continuing to educate and serve as a source of social support. The school has the role of offering the young person the knowledge necessary for learning, and a place to interact with other contexts different from the one of its family, having the opportunity to know other realities and experiences that are not propitiated by the family (Davies, 2017). The peer group, in turn, tends to increase its influence during adolescence, since the opinion and acceptance of other young people becomes an important factor for the well-being of adolescents.

In order to understand the role of these three contexts in the impulsivity of young people, it is necessary to observe the dynamics between the coexistence of these young people with the contexts and issues inherent to adolescence. Public and private schools differ in terms of teaching, structure, environment and SES. Public schools depend on government funding and, in general, lack funds to pay teachers and to maintain the environment and, in general, public education is often associated with lower socioeconomic classes while private education tends to be associated with higher socioeconomic classes. This reflects on the education and mentoring that students receive.

This difference ends up impacting on the experiences given to the students, since studies have observed that environments that provide more enriching experiences help them to better deal with neurobiological immaturity and to learn new skills (Stahmer et al., 2009; Wilson, Boyle, Yang, James, & Bennett, 2015), making them more able to cope with their impulsiveness. Further, other studies have shown that an enriched environment during childhood can assist in learning new skills and improved the cognition, communication and learning skills (Stahmer et al., 2009; Wilson et al., 2015).

Therefore, it is suggested that the environment can also be an important tool for behavioral change and this might account for less inhibitory control in preadolescents and adolescents with low SES. The medium/high SES students might have a more organized learning and enriched environment (because the quality of the environment provided in private schools), possibly with higher quality education, which may be why they show less impulsivity and greater inhibition control.

Relationship with parents can be an important protective factor for young people. From peer monitoring and school to behavioral guidance and social support that parents provide, they help young people learn to cope with impulsiveness. Studies indicate that other factors influence the impulsivity and execution of risk behaviors, such as parenting education (Arán-Filippetti & Richaud de Minzi, 2012; Auger, Lo, Cantinotti, & O'loughlin, 2010) and housing conditions of the family (Arán-Filippetti & Richaud de Minzi, 2012).

In relation to the peer group, it can be a positive and negative influence at this stage of development. When the peer group helps the young person in relation to their self-esteem, giving social support and contributing to their sense of belonging, they have a positive influence. However, this group can often negatively influence when it encourages young people to engage in risky behaviors, such as alcohol use, drug abuse, violent behavior, and law infractions of the law. In addition, by adding this influence to the normal impulsiveness of adolescence, this makes young people more likely to be influenced because they tend to act without thinking about the possible consequences of their actions. This type of influence can occur at all socioeconomic levels (DeSousa, Nuñez & De Antoni, 2014).

3. Difference in Impulsive Behaviors between Genders in Adolescence

It was possible observe that during adolescence executive functions is developing, among them the inhibition control and this develop may decrease impulsive behaviors. It also been discussed about impulsive behaviors and risk behaviors at this stage of life. What still needs to be clarified is the difference in the pattern of impulsive behavior between boys and girls.

A study evaluating inhibition control observed differences between the sexes in the relationship of inhibitory control with temperamental effortful control in young adolescents (Yücel et al., 2012). According to this same study, girls were more efficient in using strategic control to reduce the magnitude of conflicting responses when compared to boys, but it was also observed that there were no gender differences in relation to the reactive control (Yücel et al., 2012).

Another study that mentions an increase in impulsivity along the development of childhood to adolescence, followed by a decrease in these impulsive behaviors and increased inhibitory control in late adolescence also proposed results about differences between genders (Shulman, Harden, Chein, & Steinberg, 2015). The study observed higher levels of sensation seeking in boys and lower levels of impulse control compare to girls and also pointed to differences in the shapes of the developmental trajectories (Shulman et al., 2015). Adolescent girls reach a peak of sensation-seeking earlier when compared with boys, mainly because in girls this may be connected to the stage of puberty (Shulman et al., 2015). Besides, females decline in sensation-seeking more rapidly also and boys increase impulse control more gradually. The results of Shulman and colleagues' (2015) study suggested that vulnerability to risky decisions in adolescence may be greater and more intense in boys when compared to girls.

Personality, risk perception and risk taking also can be discussed within gender differences. Adolescent boys perceive their behaviors as less risky, put themselves more in risk situations, they are less sensitive to negative results and less anxious when compared to adolescent girls (Reniers, Murphy, Lin, Bartolomé, & Wood, 2016). In addition, probably the boys perception of behaviors to be less risky leads them to assume more risk and be more impulsive than girls (Reniers et al., 2016).

Despite this, it may also find different results in literature. For example, a Switzerland study found as a main result that at-risk adolescent girls displayed more externalizing symptoms, such as aggressive behavior, compared to adolescent boys (Urben et al., 2015). Besides, girls have more challenging personality traits, such as impulsivity and, no gender differences were found when comparing offenders groups (Urben et al., 2015). Another study found more psychopathic personality traits in delinquent boys when compared to the same group of girls (Stickle, Marini, & Thomas, 2012). Still in this direction, another study revealed that incarcerated adolescent girls present more internalizing problems, such as suicidal tendencies (Timmons-Mitchell et al., 1997). In community sample research, internalizing problems are usually greater in girls than boys (Stickle et al., 2012).

Although there is still divergence in the results of studies comparing gender and impulsivity or risk behavior, there is a wide diversity of studies reporting greater impulsive behavior in boys (Esteban & Tabernero, 2011; Sanchez, Rosenthal, Tansey, Frain, & Bezyak, 2016; Schaeffer et al., 2006; Whiteside & Lynam, 2001; Yücel et al., 2012). The study of Esteban and Tabernero (2011), reports a significant difference of deviant behavior in boys' classroom when compared to girls.' In addition, it was observed that one of the variables that proved relevant to predict the deviant behavior was motor impulsivity as well as cognitive factors of impulsivity (Esteban & Tabernero, 2011).

Another important issue to note is neurobiology at this stage of life, in which differences between the sexes during adolescence are also observed. Adolescent girls showed greater activation in the left ventrolateral and ventromedial prefrontal cortex, reaching into the superior temporal lobe, insula and putamen, while males showed relatively stronger activation in the right anterior cingulate/rostromedial frontal cortex, suggesting that girls were faster to inhibit their motor responses and exhibited more inhibition capacity. (Rubia et al., 2013). What is important to note is that these differences in performance and activation in brain regions happens primarily in pediatric studies (Alloway, 2012; Bezdjian, Baker, Lozano, & Raine, 2009), whereas in contrast study with adult samples no statistically significant differences were found.

CONCLUSION

This chapter aims to discuss impulsiveness in adolescence, its relationship with socioeconomic status, and gender differences. It has been reported that this period of life is marked by impulsive behaviors such as use and abuse of alcohol and drugs and that impulsive traits decrease with age because of the maturation of the prefrontal region of the brain.

It also explained about the influence of socioeconomic status on impulsivity in adolescence. Children who grow up in poverty or disadvantage live with adversity and are exposed to situations of chronic stress and risk; as a result, they have a higher prevalence of psychiatric disorders and low resilience. These stressors can affect brain systems, making cerebral maturation more susceptible to adolescence, and may have a negative impact on the development of inhibitory control and, consequently, on impulsive behaviors.

Finally, it discussed the differences between genders in the impulsive behavior and in the inhibitory control, in which an inconsistency in the literature was still observed. Despite of this, it was observed that many scientific studies have reported that there is a difference between boys and girls; among them, behavioral differences and cerebral activation. It was noticed a tendency to greater impulsivity in adolescent boys, as well as higher frequency of sensation-seeking and risk-taking. It has also been reported differences in strategies that boys and girls use, adolescents girls being more effective in using strategies to reduce conflict.

Therefore, this chapter provides insights to clarify some important points about adolescence and impulsivity, leading to the results of scientific research to support discussions. It is important to reflect on this impulsivity as behavior and as a trait in this phase of life, since impulsive or unthought behaviors are quite frequent at this stage of life. Thus, it will be possible to clarify some concepts that may aid in the understanding of issues related to adolescence.

REFERENCES

Adleman, N. E., Menon, V., Blasey, C. M., White, C. D., Warsofsky, I. S., Glover, G. H., & Reiss, A. L. (2002). A developmental fMRI study of the Stroop color-word task. *Neuroimage*, *16*(1), 61–75.

Alloway, T. P. (2012). The profile of executive function of very preterm children at 4 to 12 years. *Developmental Medicine & Child Neurology*, *54*(3), 203–204.

Arán-Filippetti, V., & Richaud de Minzi, M. C. (2012). A structural analysis of executive functions and socioeconomic status in school-age children: Cognitive factors as effect mediators. *The Journal of genetic psychology*, *173*(4), 393–416.

Aron, A. R., Fletcher, P. C., Bullmore, E. T., Sahakian, B. J., & Robbins, T. W. (2003). Stop-signal inhibition disrupted by damage to right inferior frontal gyrus in humans. *Nature neuroscience*, *6*(2), 115.

Asbridge, M., Cartwright, J., Wilson, K., & Langille, D. (2016). Age at First Drink, Experiences of Drunkenness, and Alcohol-Related Problems in Canadian Youth: Is Early Onset Bad If You Are a Moderate Drinker? *Journal of Studies on Alcohol and Drugs*, *77*(6), 974–979. https://doi.org/10.15288/jsad.2016.77.974.

Auger, N., Lo, E., Cantinotti, M., & O'loughlin, J. (2010). Impulsivity and socio-economic status interact to increase the risk of gambling onset among youth. *Addiction*, *105*(12), 2176–2183.

Barros, P. M., & Hazin, I. (2013). Avaliação das funções executivas na infância: revisão dos conceitos e instrumentos. *Psicologia em Pesquisa*, *7*(1), 13–22. [Evaluation of executive functions in childhood: review of concepts and instruments. *Psychology in Research*]

Beesdo-Baum, K., & Knappe, S. (2012). Developmental epidemiology of anxiety disorders. *Child and Adolescent Psychiatric Clinics*, *21*(3), 457–478.

Beesdo, K., Knappe, S., & Pine, D. S. (2009). Anxiety and anxiety disorders in children and adolescents: developmental issues and implications for DSM-V. *Psychiatric Clinics*, *32*(3), 483–524.

Best, J. R., Miller, P. H., & Jones, L. L. (2009). Executive functions after age 5: Changes and correlates. *Developmental review*, *29*(3), 180–200.

Bethell, C., Gombojav, N., Solloway, M., & Wissow, L. (2016). Adverse childhood experiences, resilience and mindfulness-based approaches: Common denominator issues for children with emotional, mental, or behavioral problems. *Child and Adolescent Psychiatric Clinics*, *25*(2), 139–156.

Bezdjian, S., Baker, L. A., Lozano, D. I., & Raine, A. (2009). Assessing inattention and impulsivity in children during the Go/NoGo task. *British Journal of Developmental Psychology*, *27*(2), 365–383.

Botvin, G. J., & Griffin, K. W. (2007). School-based programmes to prevent alcohol, tobacco and other drug use. *International review of psychiatry*, *19*(6), 607–615.

Carvalho Malta, D., Medeiros Mascarenhas, M. D., Lopes Porto, D., Barreto, S. M., & de Morais Neto, O. L. (2014). Exposição ao álcool entre escolares e fatores associados. *Revista de Saúde Pública*, *48*(1). Recuperado de http://www.redalyc.org/resumen.oa?id=67237023007. [Exposure to alcohol among schoolchildren and associated factors. *Journal of Public Health*]

Casey, B. J., & Jones, R. M. (2010). Neurobiology of the adolescent brain and behavior: implications for substance use disorders. *Journal of the American Academy of Child & Adolescent Psychiatry*, *49*(12), 1189–1201.

Casey, B. J., Jones, R. M., & Hare, T. A. (2008). The adolescent brain. *Annals of the New York Academy of Sciences*, *1124*(1), 111–126.

Corso, H. V., Sperb, T. M., de Jou, G. I., & Salles, J. F. (2013). Metacognição e funções executivas: relações entre os conceitos e implicações para a aprendizagem. *Psicologia: teoria e pesquisa*, *29*(1),

21–29. [Metacognition and executive functions: relationships between concepts and implications for learning. *Psychology: theory and research*]

Crone, E. A. (2009). Executive functions in adolescence: inferences from brain and behavior. *Developmental science*, *12*(6), 825–830.

Dahl, R. E., & Gunnar, M. R. (2009). Heightened stress responsiveness and emotional reactivity during pubertal maturation: implications for psychopathology. *Development and psychopathology*, *21*(1), 1–6.

Davies, B. (2017). *Life in the classroom and playground: The accounts of primary school children* (Vol. 17). Routledge.

de Almeida, R. M. M., Trentini, L. B., Klein, L. A., Macuglia, G. R., Hammer, C., & Tesmmer, M. (2014). Uso de álcool, drogas, níveis de impulsividade e agressividade em adolescentes do Rio Grande do Sul. *Psico*, *45*(1), 65–72. [Use of alcohol, drugs, levels of impulsivity and aggressiveness in adolescents from Rio Grande do Sul. *Psycho*]

Domingues, S. C. A., Mendonça, J. B., Laranjeira, R., & Nakamura-Palacios, E. M. (2009). Drinking and driving: a decrease in executive frontal functions in young drivers with high blood alcohol concentration. *Alcohol*, *43*(8), 657–664.

Esteban, A., & Tabernero, C. (2011). Relationship between impulsiveness and deviant behavior among adolescents in the classroom: age and sex differences. *Psychological Reports*, *109*(3), 703–717. https://doi.org/10.2466/02.07.09.PR0.109.6.703-717.

Ginsburg, K. R. (2007). The importance of play in promoting healthy child development and maintaining strong parent-child bonds. *Pediatrics*, *119*(1), 182–191.

Giovanelli, A., Reynolds, A. J., Mondi, C. F., & Ou, S.-R. (2016). Adverse childhood experiences and adult well-being in a low-income, urban cohort. *Pediatrics*, peds – 2015.

Hackman, D. A., & Farah, M. J. (2009). Socioeconomic status and the developing brain. *Trends in cognitive sciences*, *13*(2), 65–73.

Hare, T. A., Tottenham, N., Galvan, A., Voss, H. U., Glover, G. H., & Casey, B. J. (2008). Biological substrates of emotional reactivity and regulation in adolescence during an emotional go-nogo task. *Biological psychiatry*, *63*(10), 927–934.

Luna, B., Garver, K. E., Urban, T. A., Lazar, N. A., & Sweeney, J. A. (2004). Maturation of cognitive processes from late childhood to adulthood. *Child development*, *75*(5), 1357–1372.

Malloy-Diniz, L. F., Mattos, P., Leite, W. B., Abreu, N., Coutinho, G., Paula, J. J. de, … Fuentes, D. (2010). Translation and cultural adaptation of Barratt Impulsiveness Scale (BIS-11) for administration in Brazilian adults. *Jornal Brasileiro de Psiquiatria*, *59*(2), 99–105. [*Brazilian Journal of Psychiatry*]

Mills, K. L., Goddings, A.-L., Clasen, L. S., Giedd, J. N., & Blakemore, S.-J. (2014). The Developmental Mismatch in Structural Brain Maturation during Adolescence. *Developmental Neuroscience*, *36*(3-4), 147–160. https://doi.org/10.1159/000362328.

Moeller, F. G., Barratt, E. S., Dougherty, D. M., Schmitz, J. M., & Swann, A. C. (2001). Psychiatric aspects of impulsivity. *American journal of psychiatry*, *158*(11), 1783–1793.

Niv, S., Tuvblad, C., Raine, A., Wang, P., & Baker, L. A. (2012). Heritability and longitudinal stability of impulsivity in adolescence. *Behavior genetics*, *42*(3), 378–392.

Peeters, M., Janssen, T., Monshouwer, K., Boendermaker, W., Pronk, T., Wiers, R., & Vollebergh, W. (2015). Weaknesses in executive functioning predict the initiating of adolescents' alcohol use. *Developmental Cognitive Neuroscience*, *16*, 139–146. https://doi.org/10.1016/j.dcn.2015.04.003.

Reniers, R. L. E. P., Murphy, L., Lin, A., Bartolomé, S. P., & Wood, S. J. (2016). Risk Perception and Risk-Taking Behaviour during Adolescence: The Influence of Personality and Gender. *PLOS ONE*, *11*(4), e0153842. https://doi.org/10.1371/journal.pone.0153842.

Romer, D., Reyna, V. F., & Satterthwaite, T. D. (2017). Beyond stereotypes of adolescent risk taking: Placing the adolescent brain in developmental context. *Developmental Cognitive Neuroscience*, *27*(Supplement C), 19–34. https://doi.org/10.1016/j.dcn.2017.07.007.

Rubia, K., Lim, L., Ecker, C., Halari, R., Giampietro, V., Simmons, A., … Smith, A. (2013). Effects of age and gender on neural networks of motor response inhibition: From adolescence to mid-adulthood. *Neuro Image*, *83*, 690–703. https://doi.org/10.1016/j.neuroimage.2013.06.078.

Sacks, V., Murphey, D., & Moore, K. (2014). *Adverse childhood experiences: National and state-level prevalence.*

Sanchez, J., Rosenthal, D. A., Tansey, T. N., Frain, M. P., & Bezyak, J. L. (2016). Predicting quality of life in adults with severe mental illness: Extending the International Classification of Functioning, Disability, and Health. *Rehabilitation Psychology*, *61*(1), 19–31. https://doi.org/10.1037/rep0000059.

Sarsour, K., Sheridan, M., Jutte, D., Nuru-Jeter, A., Hinshaw, S., & Boyce, W. T. (2011). Family socioeconomic status and child executive functions: The roles of language, home environment, and single parenthood. *Journal of the International Neuropsychological Society*, *17*(1), 120–132.

Schaeffer, C. M., Petras, H., Ialongo, N., Masyn, K. E., Hubbard, S., Poduska, J., & Kellam, S. (2006). A comparison of girls' and boys' aggressive-disruptive behavior trajectories across elementary school: prediction to young adult antisocial outcomes. *Journal of consulting and clinical psychology*, *74*(3), 500.

Shirtcliff, E. A., Dahl, R. E., & Pollak, S. D. (2009). Pubertal development: correspondence between hormonal and physical development. *Child development*, *80*(2), 327–337.

Shulman, E. P., Harden, K. P., Chein, J. M., & Steinberg, L. (2015). Sex Differences in the Developmental Trajectories of Impulse Control and Sensation-Seeking from Early Adolescence to Early Adulthood. *Journal of Youth and Adolescence*, *44*(1), 1–17. https://doi.org/ 10.1007/s10964-014-0116-9.

Sinha, R. (2008). Chronic stress, drug use, and vulnerability to addiction. *Annals of the New York Academy of Sciences*, *1141*(1), 105–130.

Sowell, E. R., Thompson, P. M., Tessner, K. D., & Toga, A. W. (2001). Mapping continued brain growth and gray matter density reduction in dorsal frontal cortex: Inverse relationships during postadolescent brain maturation. *Journal of Neuroscience, 21*(22), 8819–8829.

Spear, L. (2013). The teenage brain: Adolescents and alcohol. *Current directions in psychological science, 22*(2), 152–157.

Stahmer, A. C., Hurlburt, M., Horwitz, S. M., Landsverk, J., Zhang, J., & Leslie, L. K. (2009). Associations between intensity of child welfare involvement and child development among young children in child welfare. *Child Abuse & Neglect, 33*(9), 598–611.

Stautz, K., & Cooper, A. (2013). Impulsivity-related personality traits and adolescent alcohol use: a meta-analytic review. *Clinical psychology review, 33*(4), 574–592.

Stickle, T. R., Marini, V. A., & Thomas, J. N. (2012). Gender differences in psychopathic traits, types, and correlates of aggression among adjudicated youth. *Journal of abnormal child psychology, 40*(4), 513–525.

Timmons-Mitchell, J., Brown, C., Schulz, S. C., Webster, S. E., Underwood, L. A., & Semple, W. E. (1997). Comparing the mental health needs of female and male incarcerated juvenile delinquents. *Behavioral Sciences & the Law, 15*(2), 195–202.

Turner, A. P., Hartoonian, N., Sloan, A. P., Benich, M., Kivlahan, D. R., Hughes, C.,...Haselkorn, J. K. (2016). Improving fatigue and depression in individuals with multiple sclerosis using telephone-administered physical activity counseling. *Journal of Consulting and Clinical Psychology, 84*(4), 297–309. https://doi.org/10.1037/ccp0000086.

Urben, S., Habersaat, S., Suter, M., Pihet, S., de Ridder, J., & Stephan, P. (2015). Gender differences in at risk versus offender adolescents: a dimensional approach of antisocial behavior. *Psychiatric Quarterly, 87*(4), 619–631. https://doi.org/10.1007/s11126-015-9414-y.

Verdejo-García, A., Lawrence, A. J., & Clark, L. (2008). Impulsivity as a vulnerability marker for substance-use disorders: review of findings from high-risk research, problem gamblers and genetic association studies. *Neuroscience & Biobehavioral Reviews, 32*(4), 777–810.

Whiteside, S. P., & Lynam, D. R. (2001). The five factor model and impulsivity: Using a structural model of personality to understand impulsivity. *Personality and individual differences*, *30*(4), 669–689.

Willhelm, A. R., Cabral, J. C. C., Steiger, J. O., Silva, J. F. F., Ugarte, L. M., & Almeida, R. M. M. (2015). Consumo de álcool na adolescência e relação com uso excessivo de bebidas alcoólicas dos pais: estudantes de quatro escolas de Porto Alegre. *Psico*, *46*(2), 208–216. [Alcohol consumption in adolescence and relation to excessive use of alcoholic beverages of parents: students from four schools in Porto Alegre. *Psycho*]

Wilson, R. S., Boyle, P. A., Yang, J., James, B. D., & Bennett, D. A. (2015). Early life instruction in foreign language and music and incidence of mild cognitive impairment. *Neuropsychology*, *29*(2), 292.

Yücel, M., Fornito, A., Youssef, G., Dwyer, D., Whittle, S., Wood, S. J.,…Allen, N. B. (2012). Inhibitory control in young adolescents: The role of sex, intelligence, and temperament. *Neuropsychology*, *26*(3), 347.

In: Understanding Impulsive Behavior
Editor: Christian Braddon
ISBN: 978-1-53613-815-3

Chapter 4

EMOTIONAL IMPULSIVENESS

Richard C. Howard
Institute of Mental Health, Nottingham, UK

ABSTRACT

This chapter reviews findings relating to emotional impulsiveness (EI) from the author's work and that of others. Early work is first described that identified a neural (brain-wave) signature of EI in personality disordered offenders detained in high security. It was shown that, by categorizing offenders on the basis of this brain-wave measure as *a priori* high vs. low risk and following them up following their release into the community, it was possible to predict both general and violent re-offending with a modest degree of accuracy. More recent work is then described in which, in studies of personality disordered offenders, EI has been identified as a core feature of severe PD that, in part, accounts for the link between severe personality disorder and violence. It is suggested that, viewed through the lens of a hierarchical taxonomy of psychiatric disorder, EI represents a higher-order dimension that transcends particular psychiatric diagnoses and contributes to multiple forms of psychopathology. The studies reviewed herein concern male offenders, and further studies will be required to ascertain the extent to which the findings generalize to female offenders.

INTRODUCTION

Impulsiveness refers to a predisposition to react rapidly and without planning to internal and external stimuli with little or no regard for the short-term and long-term consequences for oneself and others (Bjørkly, 2013). It is considered to be a symptom of many psychiatric disorders including borderline and antisocial personality disorders (PDs), bipolar disorder, attention deficit/hyperactivity disorder, conduct disorder, and substance abuse/dependence (Moeller, Barratt, Dougherty, Schmitz, & Swann, 2001). Impulsiveness is generally recognized to be multifaceted, incorporating a number of dimensions, including a tendency to act rashly and intemperately under the pressure of positive or negative emotions. In his early theoretical account, Shapiro (1965) regarded impulsiveness as reflecting a failure to control internal emotional impulses, and its expression as involving not just cognitive and behavioral manifestations, but affective manifestations, too. The emotionally impulsive individual responds to a stimulus or event on the basis of an immediate emotional reaction such as desire or anger, with little if any checking of long-term consequences (Wingrove & Bond, 1997).

Measures of impulsiveness, both self-report and behavioural, are limited in the degree to which they tap emotional impulsiveness. Behavioral measures of impulsiveness typically lack an emotional component, and fail to capture the essence of affectively impulsive behavior, namely the tendency to act out when in a state of heightened affect, positive or negative. Interestingly, offenders deemed at high risk of violence, even those who are clinically rated as highly impulsive, are reported to be intact so far as their *cognitive* impulse control is concerned (Bell and Polaschek, 2017). With few exceptions, for example Blackburn's (1971) impulsivity measure derived from the Minnesota Multiphasic Personality Inventory (MMPI) and the more recently described positive and negative Urgency scales from Urgency, Perseverance, Premeditation and Sensation Seeking (UPPS) scales (Whiteside & Lynam, 2001), self-report measures of impulsiveness have generally not captured the affective dimension of impulsiveness. For example, a commonly used self-report measure of impulsiveness, the Barratt Impulsivity Scales (BIS: Patton, Stanford, & Barratt, 1995) does not include an explicitly emotional component. A recent study that measured 13 indices of impulsiveness in a sample of 1252 healthy young adults found empirical support for three putatively separate domains of impulsiveness: impulsive choice, impulsive action, and impulsive personality traits, including both UPPS and BIS scales (MacKillop, Weafer, Gray, Oshri, Palmer & de Wit, 2016). However, within the personality traits domain both positive and negative Urgency from the UPPS correlated only modestly with the BIS scales (r's ranged between .31 and .42). This suggests that although not explicitly tapping emotional impulsiveness, the BIS scales – non-planning, motor, and attention - do reflect emotional impulsiveness to some, albeit limited, extent.

Another exception to the general rule that self-report measures fail to capture EI is the disinhibition component of psychopathy, operationalized by disinhibition items in the Triarchic Psychopathy Measure (TriPM: Patrick, 2010). Disinhibition describes a general phenotypic propensity toward impulse control problems entailing a lack of planfulness and foresight, *impaired regulation of affect and urges*, insistence on immediate gratification, and deficient behavioural restraint; it corresponds to a neurobehavioral dimension of inhibitory control, presumed to reflect frontal-brain-based differences in the capacity to restrain behavior and regulate affect in the service of non-immediate goals (Patrick & Drislane, 2015). Important to note is that according to Patrick and colleagues' triarchic psychopathy model (TPM), high disinhibition is not, in and of itself, diagnostic of psychopathy[1]. Similarly to EI, high disinhibition is associated with multiple overlapping conditions including attention deficit hyperactivity disorder, substance-related problems, other addictions (e.g., gambling, sex), and borderline personality disorder (Patrick, 2018).

In this chapter the author reviews findings relating to emotional impulsiveness (EI) from his own work and that of others. Early work is first described that identified a neural (brain-wave) signature of EI in personality disordered offenders detained in high security. Later, it was shown that, by

---

[1] In order to be considered a characteristic of psychopathy, high disinhibition must be accompanied by one or other of the remaining components of psychopathy, i.e., either high meanness and/or high boldness (Patrick & Drislane, 2014).

categorizing offenders on the basis of this brain-wave measure as *a priori* high vs. low risk and following them up following their release into the community, it was possible to predict re-offending with a modest degree of accuracy. More recent work is then described in which, in studies of personality disordered offenders, EI has been identified as a core feature of severe PD, and as accounting, in part, for the link between severe PD and violence (Howard, 2015). It is suggested that, within a hierarchical taxonomy of psychopathology, EI represents a higher-order construct that transcends particular psychiatric diagnoses and contributes to a broad spectrum of psychopathology.

Go/No Go Contingent Negative Variation (CNV): A Neurophysiological Index of EI

Go/No Go CNV is elicited using a behavioural paradigm in which two types of trial, Go and No Go, are randomly interleaved. On Go trials, illustrated in the upper part of Figure 1, subjects can actively avoid a burst of aversive white noise by rapidly pressing a button when the second of two successive auditory cues ("beeps") occurs. On No Go trials, shown in the lower part of Figure 1, subjects must abstain from button-pressing to the second of two successive auditory cues ("boops") on pain of receiving a burst of white noise. Typically a total of 64 trials are administered, 32 Go trials and 32 No Go trials.

As shown in Figure 2 below, the critical variable in relation to impulsiveness is the voltage *difference* between Go and No Go. Personality disordered individuals classed as emotionally impulsive by virtue of a high score on Blackburn's impulsivity measure (Blackburn, 1971) showed a lack of differentiation between Go and No Go: see bottom traces in Figure 2. This finding was replicated in emotionally impulsive and non-impulsive men recruited from the general community (Brown, Fenwick & Howard, 1989).

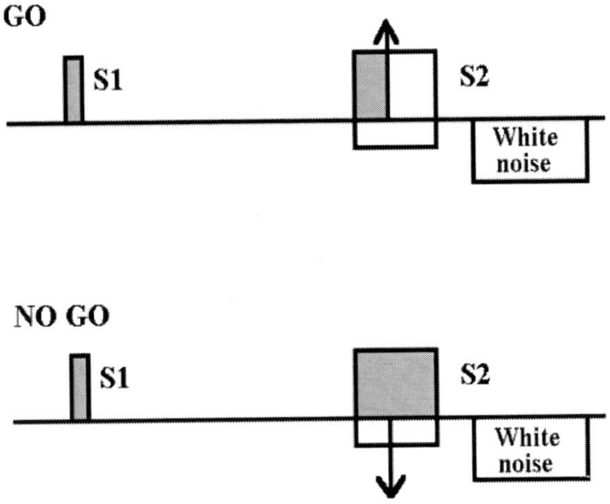

Figure 1. Behavioral paradigm for eliciting Go/No Go CNV. Arrow up/down indicates a button press to S2.

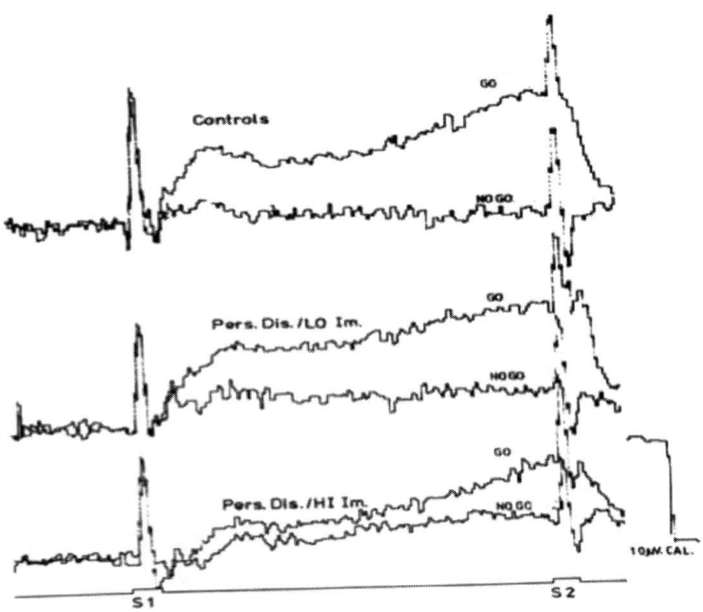

Figure 2. Go/No Go CNVs recorded from a group of healthy men (controls: top traces), male PD patients who scored low on emotional impulsiveness (middle traces: "Pers Dis/LO Im"), and male PD patients who scored high on emotional impulsiveness (bottom traces: "Pers. Dis./Hi Im."). From Howard, Fenton & Fenwick, 1982.

Three subsequent findings related to Go/No Go CNV are worthy of note. First, patients classified as *a priori* 'high-risk' or 'low risk' on the basis of their Go/No Go CNV differentiation were followed up following their release into the community. Their reconviction records were checked to see whether they had re-offended either generally or violently. Both general reoffending (Howard & Lumsden, 1996) and violent reoffending (Howard & Lumsden, 1997) were predicted with reasonable accuracy (about 70%) on the basis of poor Go/No Go CNV differentiation. As pointed out by Forde (2018), risk measures are incapable of predicting re-offending with an accuracy greater than 70%. Referring to the individual who is prone to impulsive behavior, Forde (2018, pp. 66/67) points out: "...this type of behavior is very much determined by the situation in which he finds himself. We cannot predict what situations he will get into....Therefore our ability to predict his actions will be severely limited". Consonant with this view, the current author has emphasised the importance of contextual factors, such as alcohol use and interpersonal stress, that operate as proximal causal risk factors for violence in concert with distal personality factors (Howard, 2015). In short, therefore, personality factors alone and their physiological correlates are in principle only able to predict violence with a very modest degree of accuracy.

Second, a subsequent study carried out with prisoners (Neo, McCullagh & Howard, 2001) found that the Go/No Go CNV showed a "high impulsive" pattern in those prison inmates who had a history of early-onset alcohol abuse, compared with inmates who lacked such a history. This led to the hypothesis, articulated by the present author (Howard, 2006), that early onset of alcohol abuse might account for (i.e., mediate) the progression from disordered conduct in childhood to antisocial PD and psychopathy in adulthood. The proportion of children diagnosed with childhood conduct disorder who progress to antisocial personality disorder as adults is reported to vary between 30% and 60% across different samples (Burke, Waldman & Lahey, 2010; Robins, 1978; Myers, Stewart & Brown, 1998). Howard's (2006) hypothesis was supported in two studies, one examining a North American sample of 504 young men and women recruited from the community (Howard, Finn, Gallagher & Jose, 2012), the other a sample of

100 personality disordered male offenders detained in an English high-secure hospital (Khalifa, Duggan, Howard & Lumsden, 2012). Further support for the hypothesis was provided by a study that examined the bidirectional association between changes in alcohol use and psychopathic traits across 7 annual assessments in a large sample of serious male adolescent offenders (Hawes, Crane, Henderson, Mulvey, Schubert & Pardini, 2015). Consistent with Howard's hypothesis, higher than expected levels of alcohol use at any one time point were associated with higher than expected psychopathic features at subsequent time points. A final piece of evidence that supports this hypothesis is the finding that personality disordered offenders with a high degree of psychopathic features reported a significantly greater degree of early (adolescent) alcohol abuse than did offenders who lacked psychopathic features (Varlamov, Khalifa, Liddle, Duggan & Howard, 2010). In short, these studies concur in suggesting excessive alcohol use during adolescence as a causal risk factor, in conjunction with early disordered conduct, for adult antisocial personality. A limiting factor in all these studies is that they were restricted to male offenders, thus it remains unclear whether they would generalize to female offenders. So far as psychopathy is concerned, the hypothesis would suggest that it is specifically the disinhibition component of psychopathy in Patrick's TPM, rather than boldness or meanness that is linked etiologically to early alcohol abuse and a history of childhood conduct disorder.

Does an Aberrant Go/No Go CNV Explain Criminal Reoffending?

We have noted above that an aberrant Go/No Go CNV is associated with a heightened risk of re-offending, violently and non-violently. We have good reason for thinking that Go/No Go CNV indexes EI, and that EI contributes to the risk of re-offending. However, an important *caveat* needs to be introduced in relation to the brain correlate of EI described here, a *caveat* that is exemplified by the recent discussion by Ward, Wilshire and Jackson

(2018) concerning what constitutes an adequate explanation of criminal behavior. These authors draw an important distinction between an *etiological* explanation, which "aims to depict the causal processes that result in a subsequent, downstream effect" (p. 10), and a *compositional* explanation, which "aims to describe the mechanistic components that are responsible for the occurrence of a specific phenomenon" (p. 11). Ward et al. (2018) point out that "compositional explanations in neuroscience simply describe psychological phenomena at a different level of analysis; they do not offer etiological explanations for that behaviour" (p. 19). In this sense an aberrant Go/No Go CNV does not provide an etiological explanation of EI, nor does it provide an explanation of criminal recidivism; it simply describes a neural correlate of EI that happens to predict re-offending. Nevertheless, a compositional/neuroscience explanation has three distinct advantages. First, Ward et al. point out that "neuroscience methods such as fMRI and event-related potentials generate direct markers of the brain activity occurring during a particular task, without the need for the participant to interpret that activity" (p. 15). Second, a compositional/neuroscience explanation can help in suggesting an etiological (psychological) explanation. Such was the case with the slow brain potential signature of EI described here. The chance observation that a poorly differentiated Go/No Go CNV was associated with early alcohol abuse suggested the hypothesis that such abuse was etiologically linked to the development of EI. Third, a compositional/ neuroscience explanation (e.g., "explaining" EI in terms of aberrant brain activity) can suggest targets for intervention. Such was the case when a biofeedback intervention was recently used to help a severely personality disordered, highly impulsive man to reduce his impulsiveness, both subjectively and neurophysiologically (Howard, Schellhorn & Lumsden, 2013). Clinical assessment suggested he was someone with a history of substance abuse problems who was impulsive and affectively labile, who showed rapid and extreme mood swings, with poorly controlled anger, and was suspicious and hostile in his interpersonal relationships. Following the biofeedback intervention the patient's Go/No Go CNV differentiation was substantially improved, and subjectively he reported himself to be much better able to keep control of his emotions, to think first and act later, to stop acting on impulse, and to stay out of trouble. Of course, this was just one patient, and more extensive studies will be necessary to confirm the efficacy of a biofeedback intervention to reduce EI and, perhaps more importantly, to reduce re-offending.

EMOTIONAL IMPULSIVENESS: A CORE FEATURE OF SEVERE PERSONALITY DISORDER THAT LINKS IT TO VIOLENCE

While, as noted above, most self-report measures of impulsiveness lack a clear and explicitly emotional component, a recently developed model of impulsive behavior, derived from the Five Factor Model of normal personality, conceptualizes and assesses impulsiveness as a multifaceted construct that includes four distinct and separable pathways to impulsive behavior: **U**rgency, (lack of) **P**remeditation, (lack of) **P**erseverance and **S**ensation seeking (hence it is commonly referred to by its acronym "*UPPS*"). The Urgency scale clearly and explicitly reflects negative affectivity, measuring "a tendency experience strong impulses, frequently under conditions of negative affect" (Whiteside & Lynam, 2001, p. 685). Research suggests a link between Urgency and criminality. For example, Shin, Cook, Morris, McDougle & Groves (2016) examined relationships among childhood maltreatment, UPPS impulsivity, and three types of crime, namely property crime, violent crime and fraud. Results suggested that Urgency, and by implication an inability to inhibit behavior under the influence of psychological distress, may in part account for criminality in young adults with a history of emotional abuse.

Subsequently, UPPS was revised ("*UPPS-P*") to include a positive Urgency scale to reflect impulsive behavior occurring in the context of positive affect (Lynam, Smith, Whiteside & Cyders, 2006). A recent meta-analytic review of the psychopathological correlates of UPPS scales revealed that the Negative Urgency scale demonstrated the greatest correlational effect sizes across the various forms of psychopathology examined, including alcohol/substance abuse, depression, suicidality/ nonsuicidal self-injury, aggression, anxiety, borderline personality disorder, and eating disorder (Berg, Latzman, Bliwise & Lilienfeld, 2015). Positive Urgency demonstrated a pattern of correlations similar to that of Negative Urgency, leading Berg et al. (2015) to suggest that Positive and Negative Urgency may be "…separate but closely related "subprocesses" of a broader dimension implicating strong emotion, regardless of valence, and impulsive action in response to that emotion" [p. 9]. From this meta-analytic review it can be concluded that emotional impulsiveness (Urgency) appears to be associated with a broad range of both internalizing and externalizing psychopathologies, and to reflect the intersection of internalizing and externalizing tendencies seen in severe personality disorder. A recent study by Sharp, Wright, Fowler et al. (2015) suggested a higher-order general (*g*) factor reflecting overall severity of personality disorder that cuts across different diagnostic categories and reflects both internalizing and externalizing processes, as well as cognitive disturbance (odd beliefs, ideas of reference).

A recent study of personality disordered offenders confirmed that severity of personality disorder was associated with a high level of negative Urgency (Howard & Khalifa, 2016). Severity of PD was operationalized either by combining externalizing and externalizing features or by aggregating across dimensional scores of individual personality disorders. Of all the UPPS scales, only Urgency was able to predict severity of personality disorder defined in this way. Results were consistent with those of a previous study of predominantly female patients with personality disorder (Few, Lynam & Miller, 2015). This study showed that Urgency correlated with 3 of the 5 trait domains (Negative Affectivity, Antagonism and Disinhibition) and with 14 of 25 lower-order traits included in the DSM-5 hybrid model (American Psychiatric Association, 2013). In short, therefore, a high level of emotional impulsiveness is associated with greater severity of personality disorder as indexed by a greater co-occurrence of different personality disorder categories or by the confluence of externalizing and externalizing features.

Studies further suggest that severe personality disorder and emotional impulsiveness are associated with severe violence. Among personality disordered offenders, Urgency was found to correlate significantly with a composite measure of serious violence that combined three elements: serious violence in the criminal record, early onset of violent behaviour, and serious institutional violence (Howard, Khalifa & Duggan, 2014). In essentially the same sample, severity of personality disorder, indexed by summing across personality disorder symptoms, correlated significantly with the degree of severe violence in patients' criminal records and with a younger age at onset of violent offending (Howard, Hepburn & Khalifa, 2015). Urgency also appears to be a potentially useful measure of risk of future violence. In a study of predictors of violence in psychiatric inpatients, negative Urgency in combination with having a personality disorder predicted both the number of weeks in which patients' physical aggression was observed by psychiatric nurses as well as physical aggression within the first 12 weeks of admission (Bousardt, Addriaan, Hoogendoorn, Noorthoorn, Hummeln & Nijman, 2015).

Emotional Impulsiveness Can Be Associated with Motivationally and Affectively Heterogeneous States

Thus far, EI has been considered as a relatively homogeneous construct. Likewise, violence has been considered as motivationally homogeneous, with only its severity (its impact on the victim) being considered. However, not all violence is impulsive, and the motivation for non-impulsive violence is quite different from the motivation for impulsive violence (Howard, 2011; Howard, 2015). The present author has proposed that, when it ensues in violence, emotionally driven impulsive behavior can be motivated either by the goal of achieving a heightened, hedonically positive state of excitement and exhilaration (thrill-seeking violence), or alternatively by the goal of removing a directly perceived interpersonal threat (self-protective violence). In the case of thrill-seeking violence, the violent act is triggered by a perceived opportunity to maximise pleasurable high arousal at the expense of another individual; it is *intrinsically* motivated by anticipated feelings of excitement deriving from the violent act. In the case of self-protective violence, the violent act is triggered by a perceived threat, physical or psychological, to the individual's integrity; it is *extrinsically* motivated by a desire to remove the interpersonal threat. Expressed anger, conceived as a negative hedonic state, is typically associated self-protective violence, although it has been argued that when anger is experienced as pleasant (appetitive anger: Howard, 2017a) it may be associated with thrill-seeking violence.

It is important to note that an emotionally impulsive individual may, depending on environmental contingencies and/or changes in internal state, switch rapidly between motives of excitement seeking and self-protection. For example, one may switch rapidly from a state of boredom, where one is motivated to seek excitement, to a state of anxiety where one is motivated to seek self-protection (Howard, 2011). Consistent with EI being associated with motivationally heterogeneous states, Berg et al. (2015) in their meta-analytic review of UPPS scales suggested that Urgency could be considered a broad dimension that encompasses both positive and negative affective states.

Emotional Impulsiveness Manifesting in Anger Runs Continuously through the Development of Severe Personality Disorder

Perhaps the most common concomitant of emotional impulsiveness is the experience and expression of *anger*. In a recent study of the primary emotions experienced by patients with personality disorder, anger ("feeling hotheaded, being easily irritated and frustrated, experiencing anger verbally or physically and remaining angry for long periods") emerged as the emotion that was most clearly linked to personality disorder across most categories (Karterud, Pedersen, Johansen, Wilberg, Davis & Panksepp, 2016). The experience of anger was significantly associated with paranoid, borderline, antisocial, narcissistic and obsessive-compulsive personality disorders.

Another study investigated whether measures of maladaptive schemas and modes could distinguish between three samples that were matched on gender and age: borderline PD patients, patients with other PDs, and healthy controls (Bach & Farrell, 2018). As these authors state, "schemas are viewed as underlying trait-like features of the personality whereas modes comprise fluctuating and manifest features of the personality" (p. 324), i.e., in contrast to schemas, modes are state-like variables. Three modes were shown to differentiate borderline PD patients from patients with other PDs: Angry Child ("Frequently feeling anger due to frustration of needs"), Impulsive Child ("Attempts to have a need fulfilled but done in an almost child childlike impulsive and immediate manner without considering consequences"), and Enraged Child ("A more externalized form of Angry Child involving more extreme emotions of rage often resulting in destroying objects or hurting/killing another person"). Statistical analysis using multinomial logistic regression revealed that Angry Child and Impulsive Child were significant predictors differentiating borderline PD patients from Other PD patients. The authors concluded that Angry/Enraged Child and Impulsive Child modes comprise core features of borderline PD that differentiate it from other PDs.

However, an alternative interpretation of Bach and Farrell's (2018) results is possible when one considers two points in regard to their study. First, the Angry Child and Enraged Child measures each correlated highly ($r = .65$ and $.68$ respectively) with the Impulsive Child measure. Thus it is clear that impulsiveness as operationalized in this study refers to emotional impulsiveness. Second, the BPD group, in comparison with the Other PD group, showed a pattern of comorbidity consistent with it being a more *severe* PD group than the Other PD group. The BPD group, compared with the Other PD group, contained many more individuals with paranoid PD (63% vs. 12%), antisocial PD (29% vs. 0%), narcissistic PD (7% vs. 0%), and schizotypal PD (7% vs. 0%). One quarter of the Other PD group, but none of the borderline PD group, were classified as PD - Not Otherwise Specified (PD-NOS), which is a less severe form of PD (Coccaro, Nayyer & McCloskey, 2012). Bach and Farrell's (2018) results are therefore consistent with the idea that when it co-occurs with paranoid, antisocial and narcissistic PDs, all of which are associated with excessive anger (Katerud et al., 2016), borderline PD is associated with a high level of emotional impulsiveness. In short, it was arguably emotional impulsiveness that, in Bach and Farrell's study, differentiated their borderline PD sample from their Other PD sample.

Two recent studies suggest that anger problems may be observed from a young age and are predictive of antisocial behavior and personality at later stages of development. First, a prospective study of very early (age 14 – 36 months) antecedents of childhood conduct disorder found that antisocial propensity could be identified during toddlerhood (Rhee, Friedman, Corley et al., 2016). Disregard for others (responding to others' distress with anger and hostility) was a robust predictor of conduct problems in later childhood and adolescence. Second, a propspective study delineated trajectories of anger among 503 boys using annual assessments from childhood to middle adolescence (ages 7 – 14) (Hawes, Perlman, Byrd, Raine, Loeber & Pardini, 2016). Associations between these trajectories and features of antisocial personality in young adulthood (age 28) were examined, including whether cognitive control moderates this association. As well as demonstrating considerable heterogeneity in the developmental course of anger among boys, findings from this study suggested that youth who exhibited a pattern of chronic anger beginning in childhood were at particularly high risk for displaying antisocial personality features in adulthood, but only when coupled with poor cognitive control assessed during adolescence. Taken together, results of these studies suggest that EI manifested in the propensity to experience and express anger may be an important strand that runs continuously through the developmental fabric of severe personality disorder, from early through late childhood, into adolescence and adulthood.

Where Does Emotional Impulsiveness Fit within an Hierarchical Taxonomy of Psychopathology?

Emotional impulsiveness can usefully be seen as represented at multiple levels within a hierarchical structure of psychopathology such as the Hierarchical Taxonomy of Psychopathology (HiTOP) recently proposed by Kotov et al. (2017). At the highest level of the hierarchy, that of super-spectra, EI stands as a higher-order dimension of psychopathology that is associated, at the lower level of broad spectra, with disinhibited externalizing and with aspects of internalizing (e.g., distress). At the level of syndromes/disorders, EI is associated with multiple overlapping conditions including attention deficit hyperactivity disorder, substance-related problems, other addictions (e.g., gambling, sex), and antisocial and borderline personality disorders. At the level of maladaptive traits, EI is represented by specific traits, particularly traits associated, in the Five Factor Model, with low Conscientiousness and low Agreeableness. At the lowest level in the hierarchy, symptoms and signs, EI manifests, for example, in anger-related behaviors such as hitting, shouting, attacking, etc., or in thrill-seeking behaviors such as appetitive violence.

Conclusion

Research findings reviewed here suggest that EI represents a higher-order dimension of human psychopathology that transcends particular manifestations of psychopathology. EI in adulthood has its origins in childhood temperament; it is associated with severe personality disorder, and accounts, at least in part[2], for the propensity to violence shown by those with severe personality disorder. Finally, EI has a distinct neuro-physiological signature. The studies reviewed herein primarily involved

[2] In addition to EI, other personality features are thought to contribute to violence in personality disordered individuals, in particular different facets of psychopathy (Howard, 2017b) and delusional ideation (Howard, 2015).

male offenders, and further studies will be required to ascertain the extent to which the findings generalize to female offenders.

References

American Psychiatric Association [APA]. (2013). *Diagnostic and statistical manual of mental disorders* (5th edition). Arlington, VA: Author.

Bach, B. & Farrell, J. M. (2018). Schemas and modes in borderline personality disorder: The mistrustful, shameful, angry, impulsive, and unhappy child. *Psychiatry Research, 259*, 323–329.

Bell, R. K. & Polaschek, D. L. L. (2017). Do high-risk prisoners entering treatment have clinically impaired cognitive impulse control? *Psychiatry, Psychology and Law, 24*, 576-593.

Berg, J. M., Latzman, R. D., Bliwise, N. G. & Lilienfeld, S. O. (2015). Parsing the heterogeneity of impulsivity: A meta-analytic review of the behavioral implications of the UPPS for psychopathology. *Psychological Assessment. 27*, 1129-1146.

Bjørkly, S. (2013). A systematic review of the relationship between impulsivity and violence in persons with psychosis: Evidence or spin cycle? *Aggression and Violent Behavior, 18*, 753–760.

Blackburn, R. (1971). MMPI dimensions of sociability and impulse control. *Journal of Consulting and Clinical Psychology, 37*, 166.

Bousardt, A. M. C., Addriaan, W., Hoogendoorn, A. W., Noorthoorn, E. O., Hummeln, J. W. & Nijman, H. L. I. (2015). Predicting inpatient aggression by self-reported impulsivity in forensic psychiatric patients. *Criminal Behaviour and Mental Health, 26*, 161–173.

Brown, D., Fenwick, P. B. C. & Howard, R. C. (1989). The contingent negative variation (CNV) in a Go/No Go avoidance situation: relationships with personality and subjective state. *International Journal of Psychophysiology, 7*, 35-45.

Burke, J. D., Waldman, I. & Lahey, B. B. (2010). Predictive validity of childhood oppositional defiant disorder and conduct disorder:

Implications for the DSM-V. *Journal of Abnormal Psychology*, *119*, 739-751.

Coccaro, E. F., Nayyer, H. & McCloskey, M. S. (2012). Personality disorder--not otherwise specified evidence of validity and consideration for DSM-5. *Comprehensive Psychiatry*, *53*, 907-914.

Few, L. R., Lynam, D. R. & Miller, J. D. (2015). Impulsivity-related traits and their relation to DSM–5 section II and III personality disorders. *Personality Disorders: Theory, Research, and Treatment*, *6*, 261-266.

Forde, R. A. (2018). *Bad psychology. How forensic psychology left science behind.* London/Philadelphia: Jessica Kingsley Publishers.

Hawes, S. W., Crane, C. A., Henderson, C. E., Mulvey, E. P., Schubert, C. A. & Pardini, D. A. (2015). Codevelopment of psychopathic features and alcohol use during emerging adulthood: disaggregating between- and within-person change. *Journal of Abnormal Psychology*, *124*, 729-739.

Hawes, S. W., Perlman, S. B., Byrd, A. L., Raine, A., Loeber, R. & Pardini, D. A. (2016). Chronic anger as a precursor to adult antisocial personality features. *Journal of Abnormal Psychology*. *125*, 64-67.

Howard, R. C. (2017a). Refining the Construct of 'Anger' in Relation to Personality Disorders. *Journal of Behavior*, *2*, 1013.

Howard, R. C. (2017b). Psychopathy, Impulsiveness and Violence: How are they linked? *Journal of Behavior*, *2*, 1004.

Howard, R. C. (2015). Personality disorders and violence: what is the link? *Borderline Personality Disorder and Emotion Dysregulation*, *2*, 12.

Howard, R. C. (2011). The quest for excitement: A missing link between personality disorder and violence? *Journal of Forensic Psychology and Psychiatry*, *22*, 692-705.

Howard, R. C. (2006). How is personality disorder linked to dangerousness? A putative role for early-onset alcohol abuse. *Medical Hypotheses*, *67*, 702-708.

Howard, R. C., Fenton, G. W. & Fenwick, P. B. C. (1982). *Event-related brain potentials in personality and psychopathology: A Pavlovian approach*. Letchworth, England: Research Studies Press, J Wiley & Sons.

Howard, R. C., Finn, P. R., Gallagher, J. & Jose, P. E. (2012). Adolescent-onset alcohol abuse exacerbates the influence of childhood conduct disorder on late adolescent and early adult antisocial behaviour. *Journal of Forensic Psychiatry & Psychology*, *23*, 7–22.

Howard, R. C., Hepburn, E. & Khalifa, N. (2015). Is delusional ideation a critical link in the nexus between personality disorder and violent offending? *Journal of Forensic Psychiatry and Psychology*, *26*, 368-382.

Howard, R. C. & Khalifa, N. (2016). Is emotional impulsiveness (Urgency) a core feature of severe personality disorder? *Personality and Individual Differences*, *92*, 29-32.

Howard, R. C., Khalifa, N. & Duggan, C. (2014). Antisocial personality disorder comorbid with borderline pathology and psychopathy is associated with severe violence in a forensic sample. *Criminal Behaviour and Mental Health*, *25*, 658-672.

Howard, R. C. & Lumsden, J. (1996). A neurophysiological predictor of re-offending in Special Hospital patients. *Criminal Behaviour and Mental Health*, *6*, 147-156.

Howard, R. C. & Lumsden, J. (1997). CNV predicts violent outcomes in patients released from special hospital. *Criminal Behaviour and Mental Health*, *7*, 237-240.

Howard, R. C., Schellhorn, K. & Lumsden, J. (2013). Complex case: A biofeedback intervention to control impulsiveness in a severely personality disordered forensic patient. *Personality and Mental Health*, *7*, 168-173.

Karterud, S., Pedersen, G., Johansen, M., Wilberg, T., Davis, K. & Panksepp, J. (2016). Primary emotional traits in patients with personality disorders. *Personality and Mental Health*, *10*, 261-273.

Khalifa, N., Duggan, C., Howard, R. C. & Lumsden, J. (2012). The relationship between childhood conduct disorder and adult antisocial behavior is partially mediated by early-onset alcohol abuse. *Personality Disorders: Theory, Research, and Treatment*, *3*, 423-432.

Kotov, R., Krueger, R. F., Watson, D., Achenbach, T. M., Althoff, R. R., Bagby, R. M., et al. (2017). The hierarchical taxonomy of psychopathology (HiTOP): a dimensional alternative to traditional nosologies. *Journal of Abnormal Psychology*, *26*, 454-477.

Lynam, D., Smith, G., Whiteside, S. & Cyders, M. (2006). *The UPPS-P: Assessing five personality pathways to impulsive behavior* (technical report). West Lafayette, IN: Purdue University.

MacKillop, J., Weafer, J., Gray, J., Oshri, A., Palmer, A. & de Wit, H. (2016). The latent structure of impulsivity: impulsive choice, impulsive action, and impulsive personality traits. *Psychopharmacology (Berl).* *233*, 3361–3370.

Moeller, F. G., Barratt, E. S., Dougherty, D. M., Schmitz, J. M. & Swann, A. C. (2001). Psychiatric aspects of impulsivity. *American Journal of Psychiatry*, *158*, 1783–1793.

Myers, M. G., Stewart, D. G. & Brown, S. A. (1998). Progression from conduct disorder to antisocial personality disorder following treatment for adolescent substance abuse. *American Journal of Psychiatry.*, *155*, 479-485.

Neo, L. H., McCullagh, P. & Howard, R. C. (2001). An electrocortical correlate of a history of alcohol abuse in criminal offenders. *Psychology, Crime & Law*, *7*, 105-117.

Patrick, C. J. (in press, 2018). Psychopathy as masked pathology. In C. J. Patrick (Ed.), *Handbook of psychopathy*, *2nd. Edition.* New York: Guilford Press.

Patrick, C. J. (2010). *Operationalizing the triarchic conceptualization of psychopathy: preliminary description of brief scales for assessment of boldness, meanness, and disinhibition.* Unpublished manuscript. Available from: https:// pdfs.semanticscholar.org/fb4c/ c0fdae 08405 53500ee091579ae76a6477e8e.pdf.

Patrick, C. J. & Drislane, L. E. (2015). Triarchic model of psychopathy: origins, operationalizations, and observed linkages with personality and general psychopathology. *Journal of Personality*, *83*, 627-643.

Patton, J. H., Stanford, M. S. & Barratt, E. S. (1995). Factor structure of the Barratt Impulsiveness Scale. *Journal of Clinical Psychology*, *51*, 768–774.

Rhee, S. H., Friedman, N. P., Corley, R. P., Hewitt, J. K., Hink, L. K., Johnson, D. P., Smith Watts, A. K., Young, S. E., Robinson, J., Waldman, I. D. & Zahn-Waxler, C. (2016). An examination of the developmental propensity model of conduct problems. *Journal of Abnormal Psychology*, *125*, 550-564.

Robins, L. N. (1978). Sturdy childhood predictors of adult antisocial behaviour: replications from longitudinal studies. *Psychological Medicine.*, *8*, 611-22.

Shapiro, D. (1965). *Neurotic Styles*. New York: Basic Books.

Sharp, C., Wright, A. G. C., Fowler, J. C., Frueh, B. C., Allen, J. G., Oldham, J. & Clark, L. A. (2015). The structure of personality pathology: Both general ('g') and specific ('s') factors? *Journal of Abnormal Psychology*, *124*, 387–398.

Shin, S. H., Cook, A. K., Morris, N. A., McDougle, R. & Groves, L. P. (2016). The different faces of impulsivity as links between childhood maltreatment and young adult crime. *Preventive Medicine*, *88*, 210–217. http://doi.org/10.1016/j.ypmed.2016.03.022.

Varlamov, A., Khalifa, N., Liddle, P., Duggan, C. & Howard, R. C. (2010). Cortical correlates of impaired self-regulation in personality disordered patients with traits of psychopathy. *Journal of Personality Disorders*, *25*, 74–87.

Ward, T., Wilshire, C. & Jackson, L. (2018). The contribution of neuroscience to forensic explanation. In A. R. Beech, A. J. Carter, R. E. Mann & P. Rotshtein (Eds.), *The Wiley Blackwell handbook of forensic neuroscience*. J. Wiley & Sons.

Whiteside, S. P. & Lynam, D. R. (2001). The five factor model and impulsivity: Using a structural model of personality to understand impulsivity. *Personality and Individual Differences*, *30*, 669–689.

Wingrove, J. & Bond, A. J. (1997). Impulsivity: A state as well as trait variable. Does mood awareness explain low correlations between trait and behavioural measures of impulsivity? *Personality and Individual Differences*, *22*, 333–339.

In: Understanding Impulsive Behavior
Editor: Christian Braddon
ISBN: 978-1-53613-815-3

Chapter 5

A CONCEPTUAL FRAMEWORK FOR UNDERSTANDING ALCOHOL USE PROBLEMS IN RACIAL/ETHNIC MINORITIES: THE ROLE OF IMPULSIVITY AND STRESS

Tessa Nalven*[*] *and Nichea S. Spillane
Department of Psychology, University of Rhode Island,
Kingston, RI, US

ABSTRACT

There is a robust relationship between impulsivity and alcohol use. The present review summarizes the existing literature on the influence of the dimensions of impulsivity and alcohol use problems among racial/ethnic groups. In particular, we focus on how chronic stress may influence the relationship between specific dimensions of impulsivity (e.g., negative and positive urgency) and alcohol use. While much of the existing literature has been conducted in White samples, individuals from minoritized backgrounds often deal with greater stress and stress

[*] Corresponding Author Email: tessa_nalven@my.uri.edu.

specifically related to their identity as minority (e.g., minority stress). This unique source of stress may come from sources such as perceived discrimination and living in poverty, which exposes these individuals to additional stress and has a negative impact on substance use problems. In this chapter, we will integrate the literature on impulsivity, stress, and alcohol use in minoritized groups. We propose an organizing framework for how these constructs work together to increase alcohol-related problems in members from minoritized groups and discuss the implications of this research. Additionally, we suggest there is a strong need to develop unique treatment options that are culturally and developmentally appropriate, and that target each of these constructs for members from minoritized groups.

Keywords: impulsivity, urgency, minority, stress, alcohol, emotion regulation

INTRODUCTION

Impulsivity is a widespread term that has been conceptualized in many different ways. Taking a broad approach, impulsivity can be defined as "a predisposition toward rapid, unplanned reaction to internal or external stimuli without regard to the negative consequences of these reactions" (The International Society for Research on Impulsivity, 2016). However, there has been increasing awareness and recognition that impulsivity is a multidimensional, multifaceted characteristic, with each aspect differentially related to risky and addictive behaviors (Chuang et al., 2017; Murphy, Stojek, & MacKillop, 2014). Indeed, there is a robust relationship between impulsivity and alcohol use behaviors including, heavy drinking, alcohol involvement, and alcohol-related problems (Perry & Carroll, 2008; Stamates & Lau-Barraco, 2017; Stautz & Cooper, 2013).

When compared to the general population, the prevalence of health disparities relating to Alcohol Use Disorders and problematic alcohol use is increased in many racial and ethnic minorities (Chartier & Caetano, 2010; Grant et al., 2017). This is especially true in Black (Zapolski, Pedersen, McCarthy, & Smith, 2014), (male) Hispanic, and Indigenous individuals

(Chartier & Caetano, 2010; Grant et al., 2017). Although overall alcohol use rates are highest in White individuals, Black (35.4%) and Hispanic (33.0%) individuals are more likely to have recurrent or persistent alcohol dependence when compared to White individuals (22.8%), as well as increased odds of having social consequences from drinking (Chartier & Caetano, 2010; Zapolski, et al., 2014). American Indians are more likely to engage in heavy drinking and have negative health consequences when compared to the general population (Chartier & Caetano, 2010; O'Connell, Novins, Beals, & Spicer, 2005). Additionally, when compared to White averages from a large national study (NESARC-III), American Indian men are more likely to have an alcohol use disorder (55% vs. 44%) or alcohol dependence (26% vs. 19%), and similarly women are more likely to have an alcohol use disorder (32% vs. 23%) or alcohol dependence (15% vs. 9%) (Brave Heart et al., 2016; Grant et al., 2015). In this chapter we focus on these three ethnic/racial groups. We begin by summarizing the existing literature on the relationship between impulsivity and heavy alcohol use and alcohol related problems among these minority racial/ethnic groups. We then provide a theoretical framework which theorizes that due to the additional influence of minority stress experienced by minoritized individuals, impulsivity is heightened, which in turn leads to significant alcohol use and disparities.

Problematic alcohol use includes drinking behaviors that may negatively impact an individual's social/occupational functioning; this is not always associated with high drinking volume (Lee, Rose, Engel-Rebitzer, Selya, & Dierker, 2011). Furthermore, although epidemiological studies show that many racial/ethnic groups drink less than do Whites (Chartier & Caetano, 2010), members from these groups typically demonstrate greater health disparities related to their use such as higher rates of cirrhosis, liver disease, and injuries/death from motor vehicle accidents (Centers for Disease Control and Prevention, 2013; Flores et al., 2008). These health and occupational disparities are likely due to environmental, social, and contextual factors (Centers for Disease Control and Prevention, 2013; Pedersen, Molina, Belendiuk, & Donovan, 2012).

ALCOHOL AND IMPULSIVITY

A useful framework for studying impulsivity has been the one proposed by Whiteside and Lynam in 2001, which was later refined to include an additional component of impulsivity (Cyders & Smith, 2007; Lynam, Smith, Whiteside, & Cyders, 2006). This framework has gained popularity in recent years; it describes impulsivity as consisting of five related, but distinct facets including: sensation seeking, urgency (both positive and negative), premeditation, and perseverance (Adams, Kaiser, Lynam, Charnigo, & Milich, 2012; Cyders & Smith, 2007; Cyders et al., 2009; Read, Wood, Kahler, Maddock, & Palfai, 2003; Smith et al., 2007; Whiteside & Lynam, 2001). Sensation seeking can be described as seeking out novel and exciting experiences (Stautz & Cooper, 2013; Whiteside & Lynam, 2001). Urgency is the tendency to act irrationally in response to extreme emotional positive affect (positive urgency) or negative affect (negative urgency) (Cyders & Smith, 2007; Stautz & Cooper, 2013; Whiteside & Lynam, 2001). Lack of premeditation is the tendency to not think about consequences of an action before engaging (Stautz & Cooper, 2013; Whiteside & Lynam, 2001). And lack of perseverance is the inability to maintain focus during a boring or difficult task.

Each of these facets has been found to be associated with increased alcohol use and/or problematic use (Kaiser, Bonsu, Charnigo, Milich, & Lynam, 2016; Magid & Colder, 2007). Sensation seeking is often related to high amounts of alcohol use and heavy drinking; this may be explained by positive reinforcement of the arousal caused by consuming alcohol (Cyders, et al., 2009; Fischer & Smith, 2008; Stamates & Lau-Barraco, 2017; Stautz & Cooper, 2013). Negative urgency is thought to contribute to problematic drinking due to rash responses to the experience of negative affect and therefore individuals may turn to alcohol to cope with their distress (Fischer & Smith, 2008; Stamates & Lau-Barraco, 2017). On the other hand, positive urgency is related to more alcohol use and heavy drinking, possibly in response to extreme positive affect when alcohol may be used as a celebratory means (Cyders, Flory, Rainer, & Smith, 2009; Kaiser et al., 2016; Stamates & Lau-Barraco, 2017; Stautz & Cooper, 2013). A study of college students also found a weak to medium association between positive urgency and alcohol related problems after controlling for age, gender, Greek status, and race (Labrie, Kenney, Napper, & Miller, 2014). Lack of premeditation has had mixed findings in the literature, but overall most studies determine it does have a relationship with more alcohol involvement and possibly problematic drinking behaviors (Adams et al., 2012; Fischer & Smith, 2008; Jones, Chryssanthakis, & Groom, 2014). This may be due to an individual's failure to plan out how much to drink ahead of time or what decisions to make after or during drinking (Stamates & Lau-Barraco, 2017). Finally, lack of perseverance is found to be related to alcohol use and problems with drinking, but less so than other dimensions of impulsivity; these relationships could be a function of neglect to obligations that are less amusing (Fischer & Smith, 2008; Magid & Colder, 2007; Stamates & Lau-Barraco, 2017). Overall, the different facets of impulsivity certainly relate to alcohol involvement, heavy drinking, and problems from drinking, but each may relate in different ways and amounts. However, much of the existing literature has been conducted with non-minority groups.

A small number of studies have examined some aspects of impulsivity in members from diverse ethnic/racial backgrounds. Support for the relationship between negative urgency and alcohol problems was seen in an adult group of First Nation members living in Canada (Spillane & Smith, 2010). These researchers also found that the factor structure for four of the five facets of impulsivity (positive urgency was not measured) was invariant across members from the First Nation group and White individuals (Spillane & Smith, 2010). The association between low premeditation and increased alcohol problems was also found in a study with a diverse population containing 36.8% Black/African American individuals, and the associations were not significantly different across races or gender (Latzman & Vaidya, 2013). However, further research on the facets of impulsivity and alcohol in racial minorities is lacking. This is especially important due to the findings in a study by Pedersen and colleagues (2012) which examined racial differences between White and Black Americans in the development of impulsivity and sensation seeking from childhood into adolescence and their relation to alcohol use. They found that although sensation seeking was higher for Black compared to White individuals in the sample, sensation seeking was not related to alcohol use for the Black participants. They state their results suggest that sensation seeking is at least partly responsible for early alcohol use in White individuals, but this does not necessarily hold true for other groups (Pedersen et al., 2012). This highlights that researchers cannot assume that risk factors operate in the same way for individuals of different non-White groups.

Nevertheless, this framework for understanding impulsive behavior and alcohol use warrants attention in members from other racial/ethnic backgrounds. Though there is a robust relationship between problematic alcohol use and the five aspects of impulsivity, for the purposes of this chapter, we will be focusing on the facets of impulsivity that have been found to relate to decreased emotion regulation: positive and negative urgency, due to their relationship with stress (Maxfield & Pepper, 2017; Paggeot, 2017). Cyders and Smith (2008) found these dimensions of impulsivity to be most related to emotional states and also addictive behaviors such as alcohol use.

Stress and Impulsivity

Chronic stress, or the stress response from prolonged exposure to a stimulus that has surpassed and individual's ability to cope, has been shown to be related to impulsivity and more specifically, positive and negative urgency (Hamilton, Ansell, Reynolds, Potenza, & Sinha, 2012; Hirjak et al., 2016; Perry & Carroll, 2008; Price, Connor, & Allen, 2017; Valderrama & Miranda, 2017). For example, research in young children has found that early life chronic stress is related to higher levels of impulsivity (Zhu et al., 2016), especially early life stress as the brain is still developing (Hamilton et al., 2012; Hirjak et al., 2016). Indeed, increased early life stress in children who experienced parental neglect or who were exposed to parental substance use has been associated with more impulsive behaviors (Hentges, Shaw, & Wang, 2017; Lovallo et al., 2013), as well as increased negative and positive urgency (Price et al., 2017; Valderrama & Miranda, 2017).

Minority Stress and Impulsivity

Much of the literature on stress and impulsivity has focused on White samples, therefore we know far less about how these constructs impact members from minoritized groups, who often deal with additional stressors that may cause decreased psychological well-being and associated negative health implications. Minority stress is a term used to describe the experience of stress due to an individual's membership in a stigmatized and underrepresented group (Arbona & Jimenez, 2014; Meyer, 2003; Smedley, Myers, & Harrell, 1993). This concept was originally developed in the context of sexual orientation and gender minorities, and studies found that minority stress explained increased mental health problems in minority groups due to social and environmental stressors such as stigma, discrimination, prejudice, and social stress (Meyer, 2003). The model has also been examined in minority racial and ethnic groups; Pittman and colleagues (2017) studied stress stemming from intercultural contact, which they called acculturative stress, and race-related stress, such as racial discrimination, which they found accounted for additional stress beyond general life stress. Therefore, through the experiences of discrimination, social and acculturative stress, low SES, and pressure to achieve academically, minoritized individuals are subject to uniquely additional and collective stressors related to their identities, beyond what non-minority individuals experience (Arbona & Jimenez, 2014; Lanier et al., 2017; Smedley et al., 1993). However, scarce research exists examining the direct effects of minority stress on any aspects of impulsivity, though we would hypothesize it would have an amplifying effect.

Alcohol Outcomes and Stress

Problematic alcohol behaviors have been shown to have a robust relationship with stress in existing literature (Hussong, 2003; Palmisano & Pandey, 2017); in particular when the stress is chronic (Maisto et al., 2017), and when it is experienced early in life (Gondré-Lewis et al., 2016). Early life stressors have been found to be associated with earlier initiation of alcohol use, which adds an additional risk of later life alcohol use problems (Dube et al., 2006) and dependence development (Lloyd & Turner, 2008).

Minority Stress and Alcohol

Minority stress, in particular, has been found to be associated with an increased risk for problematic alcohol use (Wilson, Gilmore, Rhew, Hodge, & Kaysen, 2016). Though most of the published research concerns minority stress in gender and sexual minoritized populations, some studies look at intersecting multiple minority identities which includes race (Keyes, Hatzenbuehler, Grant, & Hasin, 2012; Lewis, Mason, Winstead, Gaskins, & Irons, 2016; Mereish, Goldbach, Burgess, & Dibello, 2017). Additionally, Mulia and Zemore (2012) found that alcohol related disparities in racial/ethnic minorities may be a function of exposure to chronic stressors relating to social adversity and problems stemming from low SES. Pittman and colleagues (2017) utilized a minority stress framework to examine the relationship between multiple stressors and high-risk drinking behaviors in a group of second-generation, Black college students. They found a positive relationship between race-based stress and high-risk drinking behaviors and that minority stress accounted for unique variance in this relationship. Another study examining the concept of race-based traumatic stress found that Mexican American adolescents who perceived more discrimination also reported more alcohol use (Flores, Tschann, Dimas, Pasch, & de Groat, 2010). Minority stress is also related to decreased self-esteem, which has a robust relationship with increased alcohol use (Patrick & Schulenberg, 2010; Richardson, Kwon, & Ratner, 2013; Smedley et al., 1993). Therefore, minority stress is an additional stressor that adds a unique and cumulative impact on heightened problematic alcohol use.

The Circular Relationship between Stress, Impulsivity, and Alcohol

Research has also examined the relationship between stress, impulsivity, and substance use together; Perry and Carroll (2008), in a review of impulsivity and problematic drug use, found stressful and traumatic early life experiences were related to subsequent child alcohol use problems and impulsivity. Parental substance use disorder, which can be viewed as chronic stressor for a child, has also been found to predict child impulsivity which then predicted later child substance use disorder (Tarter et al., 2004). Other studies have found that the association between parent and young adult substance use was mediated by positive and negative urgency and sensation seeking; children who were abused were higher in impulsivity which in turn predicted for more substance use in young adulthood (Oshri et al., 2017). The previous research highlights the important role that chronic stress contributes to subsequent child impulsivity and substance use problems and this may occur due to parental behaviors and other early life stressors.

Furthermore, researchers have found that the relationship between stress and problematic alcohol use is influenced by impulsivity, though many of these studies look at impulsivity as a singular concept instead of examining the separate dimensions (Hamilton et al., 2012). Impulsivity mediates the relationship between stress and drinking behavior (Hamilton et al., 2012) and this relationship is reciprocal due to the nature of impulsivity acting as "both facilitator and a result of drug use" (de Wit, 2009). Quinn, Stappenbeck, and Fromme (2011) found that after accounting for the effects of individual traits, heavy drinking predicted impulsivity. A longitudinal study of alcohol use and the facets of impulsivity also found a bidirectional, reinforcing relationship; positive urgency was associated with increased alcohol use and alcohol use was associated with more positive and negative urgency, as well as increased sensation seeking and lack of premeditation (Kaiser et al., 2016). This may suggest that adolescents who are exposed to chronic stress may have increased impulsivity/positive and negative urgency which may ultimately lead to alcohol use problems; this relationship is maintained by alcohol use increasing impulsivity (see Figure 1). In the literature we reviewed we found support for all three relationships: early life stress relates to impulsivity, stress relates to alcohol use, and impulsivity and alcohol use also have a strong and reciprocal relationship.

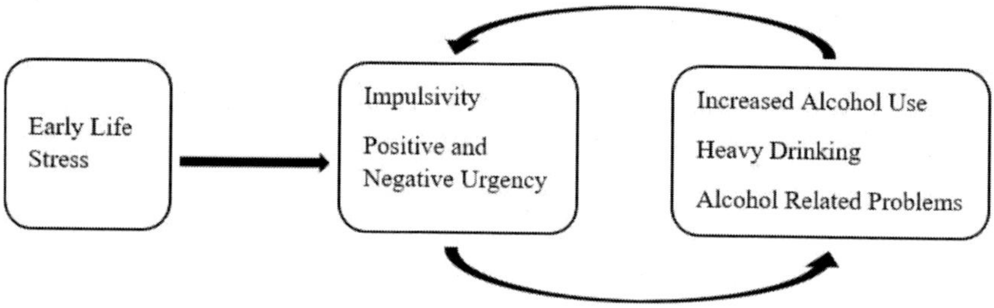

Figure 1. Conceptual model for understanding the relationship from stress to problematic alcohol use through impulsivity.

However, members from minoritized groups tend to experience more stress in addition to the everyday stress experienced by most people. Because of the additional stress, positive and negative urgency may be heightened for those individuals. Due to the circular and reciprocal relationships between stress, impulsivity, and alcohol use/problems, minority stress has a unique additional impact on the development of increased problematic alcohol use and impulsivity. Research suggests this may be true; Andrade and Petry (2014) found impulsive behavior was more prominent in African American and Hispanic participants when compared to White individuals. In addition, Latzman, Chan, and Shishido (2013) found that the link between racial discrimination and problematic alcohol use is moderated by impulsivity, most strongly with the positive urgency and lack of premeditation facets. The cycle is additionally reinforced by parental substance use (and related child neglect and abuse), which increases the exposure to stressors in the adolescent's life. Barriers to proper care (e.g., low SES), peer substance use due to similar pathways, and poor social support add to the health disparities among minoritized groups, which prevents the cycle from being broken (see Figure 2).

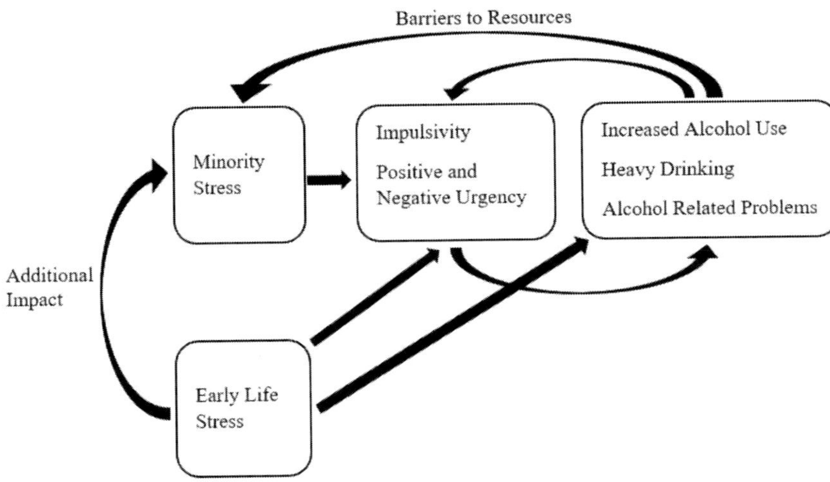

Figure 2. Conceptual model of minority stress' impact on problematic alcohol use through impulsivity.

CONCLUSION

Based on our review of the literature, we conclude that minority stress is a unique form of stress that is distinguishable from other types of stressors (Meyer, 2003; Pittman et al., 2017). It therefore may contribute to a cycle of alcohol use problems in minoritized groups who experience health and alcohol use disparities due to the social and environmental influences. This may lead to heightened levels of negative and positive urgency, which in turn leads to increased problematic alcohol use (Bountress et al., 2017). Additionally, the experience of parental neglect and abuse combined with a lack of resources to prevent problematic alcohol use contributes to the cycle. Those children may be at greater risk of then perpetuating the cycle of abuse and neglect (Dube et al., 2001).

Early stressful experiences such as those mentioned above are important during adolescent developmental period, which is a period of time when impulsivity and positive and negative urgency are at their peak (Stautz & Cooper, 2013). Some studies suggest that heightened impulsivity and emotion regulation difficulties in adolescents can be partially explained by an underdeveloped frontal cortex of the brain (Gullo & Dawe, 2008; Hirjak et al., 2016; Schilling et al., 2012). This impairment in the frontal cortex can be, in part, explained by significant youth stress (Hirjak et al., 2016; Lu & Richardson, 2014). Interestingly, alcohol use can also cause changes to the prefrontal cortex that are thought to contribute to the maintenance of addictive behaviors (Lu & Richardson, 2014). For example, Whelan and colleagues (2012) found an association between hypofunctioning frontal cortices, impulsivity, and initiation of alcohol use in adolescents. Therefore, high levels of stress in adolescents of minority groups, in particular, could be associated with and partially explained by increased negative and positive urgency. As previously mentioned above, positive and negative urgency are associated with increased alcohol use, heavy drinking, and problematic alcohol behaviors (Cyders et al., 2009). In turn, the increased alcohol involvement amplifies impulsivity, which continues the cycle. Consistent with this view, research by Rogers and colleagues (2017) found that not all minoritized individuals experiencing minority stress have increased problematic alcohol use, but that greater levels of minority stress predict greater levels of emotion regulation difficulties which in turn is related to alcohol use. Individuals struggling with emotion regulation are likely high in the positive and negative urgency aspects of impulsivity (Maxfield & Pepper, 2017; Paggeot, 2017).

Should support for this theory be found, the implications would be to develop unique treatment options that are culturally and developmentally appropriate for members from minoritized groups. Prevention programs should especially target young members of minoritized groups who are more likely to experience heightened stress. Furthermore, the way an individual copes with stress may impact the relationship between stress and alcohol use (Veenstra et al., 2007). For example, researchers examined the role coping strategies play in a large, multiethnic study and found that both avoidance-oriented and social support-based coping strategies were associated with more alcohol consumption (Aldridge-Gerry et al., 2011). However, these relationships are not consistent across ethnicities, such that, African Americans were more likely to use religious coping strategies whereas social support as a coping strategy was associated with more alcohol use among

Asian Americans (Aldridge-Gerry et al., 2011). These results suggest that the effectiveness of coping strategies and cultural context can vary across groups. Therefore, to be successful in applying coping strategies to reduce alcohol use, we must be aware of culturally appropriate strategies. Having stimulating activities available could be a potential prevention/intervention strategy for regulating the emotional experience youth express. To the extent that adolescents see available alternative options and engage in non-substance related activities, they may be positively reinforced and less inclined to use alcohol. These ideas are consistent with the hypotheses derived from the Behavioral Theories of Choice (Vuchinich & Tucker, 1988). Additionally, having positive role models leading activities and engaging cultural climates may prove to be useful in prevention/intervention strategies. This could be especially effective for those who are high in positive and negative urgency as it relates to their emotion regulation.

Furthermore, we would suggest that this is a multifaceted problem that could benefit from a multilevel intervention. Other important factors to consider include barriers to treatment that may include stigma, discrimination, access to treatment, low SES, and social adversity, which are also significant causes of stress in many minority individuals' lives. Large scale societal education and training around intentional and unintentional prejudice, as well as cultural competence training for clinicians need to be emphasized in order to make meaningful changes. Community mental health awareness and reduction of stigma for mental healthcare among minoritized groups may also help end the cycle of aversive childhood events leading to subsequent negative health and alcohol disparities.

REFERENCES

Adams, Z. W., Kaiser, A. J., Lynam, D. R., Charnigo, R. J. & Milich, R. (2012). Drinking motives as mediators of the impulsivity-substance use relation: Pathways for negative urgency, lack of premeditation, and sensation seeking. *Addictive Behaviors*, *37*(7), 848-855. doi: 10.1016/ j.addbeh.2012.03.016.

Aldridge-Gerry, A. A., Roesch, S. C., Villodas, F., McCabe, C., Leung, Q. K. & Da Costa, M. (2011). Daily Stress and Alcohol Consumption: Modeling Between-Person and Within-Person Ethnic Variation in Coping Behavior. *Journal of Studies on Alcohol and Drugs*, *72*(1), 125–134.

Andrade, L. F. & Petry, N. M. (2014). White problem gamblers discount delayed rewards less steeply than their African American and Hispanic counterparts. *Psychology of Addictive Behaviors*, *28*(2), 599-606. doi: http://dx.doi.org.uri.idm.oclc.org/10.1037/a0036153.

Arbona, C. & Jimenez, C. (2014). Minority stress, ethnic identity, and depression among Latino/a college students. *Journal of Counseling Psychology*, *61*(1), 162-168. doi: 10.1037/a0034914.

Bountress, K., Adams, Z. W., Gilmore, A. K., Amstadter, A. B., Thomas, S. & Danielson, C. K. (2017). Associations among impulsivity, trauma history, and alcohol misuse within a young adult sample. *Addictive Behaviors*, 64, 179-184. doi: 10.1016/j.addbeh.2016.08.031.

Brave Heart, M. H., Lewis-Fernández, R., Beals, J., Hasin, D. S., Sugaya, L., Wang, S. & Blanco, C. (2016). Psychiatric disorders and mental health treatment in American Indians and Alaska Natives: Results of the National Epidemiologic Survey on Alcohol and Related Conditions. *Social Psychiatry and Psychiatric Epidemiology*, *51*(7), 1033-1046. doi: 10.1007/s00127-016-1225-4.

Centers for Disease Control and Prevention. (2013). CDC health disparities and inequalities report: United States, 2013. *Morbidity and Mortality Weekly Report*, *62*(3, Supplement). Retrieved from https:// www.cdc.gov/mmwr/pdf/other/su6203.pdf.

Chartier, K. & Caetano, R. (2010). Ethnicity and Health Disparities in Alcohol Research. Alcohol Research & Health : *The Journal of the National Institute on Alcohol Abuse and Alcoholism*, *33*(1-2), 152–160.

Chuang, C. I., Sussman, S., Stone, M. D., Pang, R. D., Chou, C., Leventhal, A. M. & Kirkpatrick, M. G. (2017). Impulsivity and history of behavioral addictions are associated with drug use in adolescents. *Addictive Behaviors*, *74*, 41-47. doi: 10.1016/j.addbeh.2017.05.021.

Cyders, M. A., Flory, K., Rainer, S. & Smith, G. T. (2009). The role of personality dispositions to risky behavior in predicting first-year college drinking. *Addiction*, *104*(2), 193-202. doi: 10.1111/j.1360-0443.2008.02434.x.

Cyders, M. A. & Smith, G. T. (2007). Mood-based rash action and its components: Positive and negative urgency. *Personality and Individual Differences*, *43*(4), 839-850. doi: 10.1016/j.paid. 2007. 02.008.

Cyders, M. A. & Smith, G. T. (2008). Emotion-based Dispositions to Rash Action: Positive and Negative Urgency. *Psychological Bulletin*, *134*(6), 807–828. http://doi.org/10.1037/a0013341.

De Wit, H. (2009). Impulsivity as a determinant and consequence of drug use: a review of underlying processes. *Addiction Biology*, *14*(1), 22–31. http://doi.org/10.1111/j.1369-1600.2008.00129.x.

Dube, S. R., Anda, R. F., Felitti, V. J., Croft, J. B., Edwards, V. J. & Giles, W. H. (2001). Growing up with parental alcohol abuse. *Child Abuse & Neglect*, *25*(12), 1627-1640. doi: 10.1016/s0145-2134(01)00293-9.

Dube, S. R., Miller, J. W., Brown, D. W., Giles, W. H., Felitti, V. J., Dong, M. & Anda, R. F. (2006). Adverse childhood experiences and the association with ever using alcohol and initiating alcohol use during adolescence. *Journal of Adolescent Health*, *38*(4). doi: 10.1016/j.jadohealth.2005.06.006.

Flores, E., Tschann, J. M., Dimas, J. M., Pasch, L. A. & de Groat, C. L. (2010). Perceived racial/ethnic discrimination, posttraumatic stress symptoms, and health risk behaviors among Mexican American adolescents. *Journal of Counseling Psychology*, *57*(3), 264-273. doi: 10.1037/a0020026.

Flores, Y. N., Yee, H. F., Leng, M., Escarce, J. J., Bastani, R., Salmerón, J. & Morales, L. S. (2008). Risk Factors for Chronic Liver Disease in Blacks, Mexican Americans, and Whites in the United States: Results From NHANES IV, 1999-2004. *The American Journal of Gastroenterology*, *103*(9), 2231-2238. doi: 10.1111/j.1572-0241.2008.02022.x.

Fischer, S. & Smith, G. T. (2008). Binge eating, problem drinking, and pathological gambling: Linking behavior to shared traits and social learning. *Personality and Individual Differences*, *44*(4), 789-800. doi: 10.1016/j.paid.2007.10.008.

Gondré-Lewis, M. C., Warnock, K. T., Wang, H., June, H. J., Bell, K. A., Rabe, H. & June, H. S. (2016). Early life stress is a risk factor for excessive alcohol drinking and impulsivity in adults and is mediated via a CRF/GABAA mechanism. Stress: *The International Journal on The Biology of Stress*, *19*(2), 235-247. doi: 10.3109/ 10253890. 2016. 1160280.

Gullo, M. & Dawe, S. (2008). Impulsivity and adolescent substance use: Rashly dismissed as "all-bad"? *Neuroscience & Biobehavioral Reviews*, *32*(8), 1507-1518. doi: 10.1016/j.neubiorev.2008.06.003.

Grant, B. F., Chou, S. P., Saha, T. D., Pickering, R. P., Kerridge, B. T., Ruan, W. J. & Hasin, D. S. (2017). Prevalence of 12-Month Alcohol Use, High-Risk Drinking, and DSM-IV Alcohol Use Disorder in the United States, 2001-2002 to 2012-2013. *JAMA Psychiatry*, *74*(9), 911. doi: 10.1001/jamapsychiatry.2017.2161.

Grant, B. F., Goldstein, R. B., Saha, T. D., Chou, S. P., Jung, J., Zhang, H., & Hasin, D. S. (2015). Epidemiology of DSM-5 alcohol use disorder: Results from the National Epidemiologic Survey on Alcohol and Related Conditions III. *JAMA Psychiatry*, *72*(8), 757-766. doi: 10.1001/jamapsychiatry.2015.0584.

Hamilton, K. R., Ansell, E. B., Reynolds, B., Potenza, M. N. & Sinha, R. (2012). Self-reported impulsivity, but not behavioral choice or response impulsivity, partially mediates the effect of stress on drinking behavior. *Stress*, *16*(1), 3-15. doi: 10.3109/10253890.2012.671397.

Hentges, R., Shaw, D. & Wang, M. (2017). Early childhood parenting and child impulsivity as precursors to aggression, substance use, and risky sexual behavior in adolescence and early adulthood. *Development and Psychopathology*, 1-15. doi: 10.1017/S0954579417001596.

Hirjak, D., Thomann, A. K., Kubera, K. M., Wolf, R. C., Jeung, H., Maier-Hein, K. H. & Thomann, P. A. (2016). Cortical folding patterns are associated with impulsivity in healthy young adults. *Brain Imaging and Behavior*, *11*(6), 1592-1603. doi: 10.1007/s11682-016-9618-2.

Hussong, A. M. (2003). Further refining the stress-coping model of alcohol involvement. *Addictive Behaviors*, *28*(8), 1515-1522. doi: 10.1016/S0306-4603(03)00072-8.

Jones, K. A., Chryssanthakis, A. & Groom, M. J. (2014). Impulsivity and drinking motives predict problem behaviours relating to alcohol use in University students. *Addictive Behaviors*, *39*(1), 289-296. doi: 10.1016/j.addbeh.2013.10.024.

Kaiser, A., Bonsu, J. A., Charnigo, R. J., Milich, R. & Lynam, D. R. (2016). Impulsive Personality and Alcohol Use: Bidirectional Relations Over One Year. *Journal of Studies on Alcohol and Drugs*, *77*(3), 473-482. doi: 10.15288/jsad.2016.77.473.

Keyes, K., Hatzenbuehler, M., Grant, B. F. & Hasin, D. S. (2012). Stress and Alcohol: Epidemiologic Evidence. Alcohol Research: *Current Reviews*, *34*(4), 391–400.

Labrie, J. W., Kenney, S. R., Napper, L. E. & Miller, K. (2014). Impulsivity and alcohol-related risk among college students: Examining urgency, sensation seeking and the moderating influence of beliefs about alcohols role in the college experience. *Addictive Behaviors*, *39*(1), 159-164. doi: 10.1016/j.addbeh.2013.09.018.

Lanier, Y., Sommers, M. S., Fletcher, J., Sutton, M. Y. & Roberts, D. D. (2017). Examining racial discrimination frequency, racial discrimination stress, and psychological well-being among Black early adolescents. *Journal of Black Psychology*, *43*(3), 219-229. doi: 10.1177/0095798416638189.

Latzman, R. D., Chan, W. Y. & Shishido, Y. (2013). Impulsivity moderates the association between racial discrimination and alcohol problems. *Addictive Behaviors*, *38*(12), 2898-2904. doi: 10.1016/j.addbeh.2013.08.020.

Latzman, R. D. & Vaidya, J. G. (2013). Common and distinct associations between aggression and alcohol problems with trait disinhibition. *Journal of Psychopathology and Behavioral Assessment*, *35*(2), 186-196. doi: 10.1007/s10862-012-9330-5.

Lee, C., Rose, J. S., Engel-Rebitzer, E., Selya, A. & Dierker, L. (2011). Alcohol dependence symptoms among recent onset adolescent drinkers.

Addictive Behaviors, *36*(12), 1160-1167. doi: 10.1016/j.addbeh.2011.07.014.

Lewis, R. J., Mason, T. B., Winstead, B. A., Gaskins, M. & Irons, L. B. (2016). Pathways to hazardous drinking among racially and socioeconomically diverse lesbian women: Sexual minority stress, rumination, social isolation, and drinking to cope. *Psychology of Women Quarterly*, *40*(4), 564-581. doi: 10.1177/0361684316662603.

Lloyd, D. A. & Turner, R. J. (2008). Cumulative lifetime adversities and alcohol dependence in adolescence and young adulthood. *Drug and Alcohol Dependence*, *93*(3), 217-226. doi: 10.1016/j.drugalcdep.2007.09.012.

Lovallo, W. R., Farag, N. H., Sorocco, K. H., Acheson, A., Cohoon, A. J. & Vincent, A. S. (2013). Early Life Adversity Contributes to Impaired Cognition and Impulsive Behavior: Studies from the Oklahoma Family Health Patterns Project. *Alcoholism, Clinical and Experimental Research*, *37*(4), 616–623. http://doi.org/10.1111/acer.12016.

Lu, Y. & Richardson, H. (2014). Alcohol, stress hormones, and the prefrontal cortex: A proposed pathway to the dark side of addiction. *Neuroscience*, *277*, 139-151. doi: 10.1016/j.neuroscience.2014.06.053.

Lynam, D. R., Smith, G. T., Whiteside, S. P. & Cyders, M. A. (2006). *The UPPS-P: Assessing five personality pathways to impulsive behavior (technical report)*. West Lafayette, IN: Purdue University.

Magid, V. & Colder, C. R. (2007). The UPPS Impulsive Behavior Scale: Factor structure and associations with college drinking. *Personality and Individual Differences*, *43*(7), 1927-1937. doi: 10.1016/j.paid.2007.06.013.

Maisto, S. A., Xie, F. C., Witkiewitz, K., Ewart, C. K., Connors, G. J., Zhu, H. & Chow, S. (2017). How chronic self-regulatory stress, poor anger regulation, and momentary affect undermine treatment for alcohol use disorder: Integrating social action theory with the dynamic model of relapse. *Journal of Social and Clinical Psychology*, *36*(3), 238-263. doi: 10.1521/jscp.2017.36.3.238.

Mereish, E. H., Goldbach, J. T., Burgess, C. & Dibello, A. M. (2017). Sexual orientation, minority stress, social norms, and substance use among racially diverse adolescents. *Drug and Alcohol Dependence*, *178*, 49-56. doi: 10.1016/j.drugalcdep.2017.04.013.

Meyer, I. H. (2003). Prejudice, social stress, and mental health in lesbian, gay, and bisexual populations: Conceptual issues and research evidence. *Psychological Bulletin*, *129*(5), 674-697. doi: 10.1037/0033-2909.129.5.674.

Mulia, N. & Zemore, S. E. (2012). Social Adversity, Stress, and Alcohol Problems: Are Racial/Ethnic Minorities and the Poor More Vulnerable? *Journal of Studies on Alcohol and Drugs*, *73*(4), 570-580. doi: 10.15288/jsad.2012.73.570.

Murphy, C. M., Stojek, M. K. & Mackillop, J. (2014). Interrelationships among impulsive personality traits, food addiction, and Body Mass Index. *Appetite*, *73*, 45-50. doi: 10.1016/j.appet.2013.10.008.

O'Connell, J. M., Novins, D. K., Beals, J. & Spicer, P. (2005). Disparities in Patterns of Alcohol Use Among Reservation-based and Geographically Dispersed American Indian Populations. Alcoholism: *Clinical & Experimental Research*, *29*(1), 107-116. doi: 10.1097/01.alc.0000153789.59228.fc.

Oshri, A., Kogan, S., Kwon, J., Wickrama, K., Vanderbroek, L., Palmer, A. & MacKillop, J. (2017). Impulsivity as a mechanism linking child abuse and neglect with substance use in adolescence and adulthood. *Development and Psychopathology*, 1-19. doi: 10.1017/ S0954579417 000943.

Paggeot, A. (2017). Understanding urgency in borderline personality disorder: Disinhibition or impulsive emotion regulation? [Abstract]. *Dissertation Abstracts International*, *78*(3-B), E. (Accession No. 2017-05714-034).

Palmisano, M. & Pandey, S. C. (2017). Epigenetic mechanisms of alcoholism and stress-related disorders. *Alcohol*, *60*, 7-18. doi: 10.1016/ j.alcohol.2017.01.001.

Pedersen, S. L., Molina, B. S., Belendiuk, K. A. & Donovan, J. E. (2012). Racial Differences in the Development of Impulsivity and Sensation Seeking from Childhood into Adolescence and Their Relation to

Alcohol Use. Alcoholism: *Clinical and Experimental Research*, *36*(10), 1794-1802. doi: 10.1111/j.1530-0277.2012.01797.x.

Perry, J. L. & Carroll, M. E. (2008). The role of impulsive behavior in drug abuse. *Psychopharmacology*, *200*(1), 1-26. doi: 10.1007/s00213-008-1173-0.

Pittman, D. M., Cho Kim, S., Hunter, C. D. & Obasi, E. M. (2017). The role of minority stress in second-generation Black emerging adult college students' high-risk drinking behaviors. *Cultural Diversity and Ethnic Minority Psychology*, *23*(3), 445-455. doi: 10.1037/cdp0000135.

Price, M., Connor, J. P. & Allen, H. C. (2017). The moderating effect of childhood maltreatment on the relations among PTSD symptoms, positive urgency, and negative urgency. *Journal of Traumatic Stress*, *30*(4), 432-437. doi: 10.1002/jts.22198.

Quinn, P. D., Stappenbeck, C. A. & Fromme, K. (2011). Collegiate heavy drinking prospectively predicts change in sensation seeking and impulsivity. *Journal of Abnormal Psychology*, *120*(3), 543-556. doi: 10.1037/a0023159.

Read, J. P., Wood, M. D., Kahler, C. W., Maddock, J. E. & Palfai, T. P. (2003). Examining the role of drinking motives in college student alcohol use and problems. *Psychology of Addictive Behaviors*, *17*(1), 13-23. doi: 10.1037/0893-164x.17.1.13\.

Richardson, C. G., Kwon, J. Y. & Ratner, P. A. (2013). Self-esteem and the initiation of substance use among adolescents. *Canadian journal of public health*, *104*(1), e60-e63.

Schilling, C., Kühn, S., Paus, T., Romanowski, A., Banaschewski, T., Barbot, A. & Gallinat, J. (2012). Cortical thickness of superior frontal cortex predicts impulsiveness and perceptual reasoning in adolescence. *Molecular Psychiatry*, *18*(5), 624-630. doi: 10.1038/ mp.2012.56.

Smedley, B. D., Myers, H. F. & Harrell, S. P. (1993). Minority-Status Stresses and the College Adjustment of Ethnic Minority Freshmen. *The Journal of Higher Education*, *64*(4), 434. doi: 10.2307/2960051.

Smith, G. T., Fischer, S., Cyders, M. A., Annus, A. M., Spillane, N. S. & Mccarthy, D. M. (2007). On the Validity and Utility of Discriminating

Among Impulsivity-Like Traits. *Assessment*, *14*(2), 155-170. doi: 10.1177/1073191106295527.

Spillane, N. S. & Smith, G. T. (2010). Individual differences in problem drinking among tribal members from one first nation community. *Alcoholism: Clinical and Experimental Research*, *34*(11), 1985-1992. doi: 10.1111/j.1530-0277.2010.01288.x.

Stamates, A. L. & Lau-Barraco, C. (2017). The dimensionality of impulsivity: Perspectives and implications for emerging adult drinking. *Experimental and Clinical Psychopharmacology*, *25*(6), 521-533. doi: 10.1037/pha0000153.

Stautz, K. & Cooper, A. (2013). Impulsivity-related personality traits and adolescent alcohol use: A meta-analytic review. *Clinical Psychology Review*, *33*(4), 574-592. doi: 10.1016/j.cpr.2013.03.003.

Tarter, R. E., Kirisci, L., Habeych, M., Reynolds, M. & Vanyukov, M. (2004). Neurobehavior disinhibition in childhood predisposes boys to substance use disorder by young adulthood: direct and mediated etiologic pathways. *Drug and Alcohol Dependence*, *73*(2), 121-132. doi: 10.1016/j.drugalcdep.2003.07.004.

The International Society for Research on Impulsivity. (2016). *What is impulsivity?* Retrieved from http://www.impulsivity.org/.

Valderrama, J. & Miranda, R. (2017). Early life stress predicts negative urgency through brooding, depending on 5-HTTLPR genotype: A pilot study with 6-month follow-up examining suicide ideation. *Psychiatry Research*, *258*, 481-487. doi: 10.1016/j.psychres.2017.08.092.

Veenstra, M. Y., Lemmens, P. H., Friesema, I. H., Tan, F. E., Garretsen, H. F., Knottnerus, J. A. & Zwietering, P. J. (2007). Coping style mediates impact of stress on alcohol use: A prospective population-based study. *Addiction*, *102*(12), 1890-1898. doi: 10.1111/j.1360-0443.2007.02026. x.

Vuchinich, R. E. & Tucker, J. A. (1988). Contributions from behavioral theories of choice to an analysis of alcohol abuse. *Journal of Abnormal Psychology*, *97*(2), 181.

Whelan, R., Conrod, P. J., Poline, J. B., Lourdusamy, A., Banaschewski, T., Barker, G. J. & Consortium, I. (2012). Adolescent impulsivity phenotypes characterized by distinct brain networks. *Nature Neuroscience*, *15*(6), 920–925. doi: 10.1038/nn.3092.

Whiteside, S. P. & Lynam, D. R. (2001). The Five Factor Model and impulsivity: using a structural model of personality to understand impulsivity. *Personality and Individual Differences*, *30*(4), 669-689. doi: 10.1016/s0191-8869(00)00064-7.

Wilson, S. M., Gilmore, A. K., Rhew, I. C., Hodge, K. A. & Kaysen, D. L. (2016). Minority stress is longitudinally associated with alcohol-related problems among sexual minority women. *Addictive Behaviors*, *61*, 80-83. doi: 10.1016/j.addbeh.2016.05.017.

Zhu, H., Luo, X., Cai, T., He, J., Lu, Y. & Wu, S. (2016). Life event stress and binge eating among adolescents: The roles of early maladaptive schemas and impulsivity. *Stress and Health: Journal of The International Society for The Investigation of Stress*, *32*(4), 395-401. doi: 10.1002/smi.2634.

In: Understanding Impulsive Behavior
Editor: Christian Braddon
ISBN: 978-1-53613-815-3

Chapter 6

Childhood Impulsive Behavior and Problem Gambling by Adulthood: An Update on a 30-Year Prospective Community-Based Investigation

Edmond D. Shenassa[1,2,*], Angela D. Paradis[2] and Stephen L. Buka[2]
[1]Maternal and Child Health Program, Department of Family Science, School of Public Health, University of Maryland, College Park, MD, US
[2]Department of Epidemiology, Brown School of Public Health, Providence, RI, US

Abstract

We prospectively investigated the association between impulsive behaviors at age 7 and the development of problem gambling by adulthood.

* Corresponding Author: Edmond D. Shenassa, ScD, Maternal and Child Health Program, 1142Z School of Public Health, College Park, Maryland 20742. Email: Shenassa@UMD.edu.

To determine the specificity of any observed association between impulsive behaviors and problem gambling we also examined the link between respondents' shy/depressed behaviors in childhood and later problem gambling.

Our study participants were 958 offspring of mothers enrolled in the Collaborative Perinatal Project who participated in an adult follow-up study at a mean age of 39 years. Multivariable logistic regression models were fit to determine associations between psychologist-rated impulsive and shy/depressed behaviors at age 7 and self-reported gambling as measured by the South Oaks Gambling Screen administered during the adult follow-up study.

We found that children who exhibited impulsive behaviors at age 7, compared to their non-impulsive counterparts, were 3.24 (95% confidence interval: 1.47-7.14) times more likely to report problem gambling during adulthood. In contrast, we did not find a significant association between childhood shy/depressed behavior and problem gambling by adulthood in adjusted analyses. In conclusion, our longitudinal investigation found prospective evidence that impulsive behaviors at age 7 are a specific and significant risk factor for later problem gambling.

Keywords: impulsive behavior, shy/depressed behavior, gambling, longitudinal

INTRODUCTION

Since publication of our longitudinal study of impulsivity during childhood and risk of problem gambling by adulthood [1], interest in better understanding problem gambling has grown exponentially [2]. Social and personal implications of problem gambling, characterized by gambling in spite of psychosocial problems as well as legal and financial problems [3, 4], has come into clear relief in tandem with growth of the gaming industry which has continued unabated since gambling was first legalized in Nevada in 1931 [4–6]. The significant health and social problems associated with problem gambling underscore the need to identify its early pre-cursors.

Among risk factors for problem gambling, various manifestations of impulsivity figure prominently. Laboratory studies have consistently found problem gamblers to exhibit diminished functioning within areas of brain, such as the anterior cingulate cortex and the frontal cortex, that are believed to control cognitive and motivational functions [7]. These findings are also supported by psychological investigations which have found behavioral and cognitive impulsivity to be a key characteristic of adult problem gamblers [8–14]. Two meta-analyses have found reasonably robust differences between problem gamblers and others across various manifestations of impulsivity. A meta-analysis of 44 studies comparing problem gamblers with non-pathological gamblers found that problem gamblers are likely to have deficiencies in impulse control that fit within a broader constellation of externalizing behaviors [15]. A meta-analysis of 20 studies, focused exclusively on problem gamblers without comorbid substance use disorders, found that compared to healthy controls problem gamblers are deficient in executive cognitive control. More specifically, this meta-analysis found motor impulsivity, and to lesser extent deficits in sustained attention, to be prominent features among problem gamblers, accounting for poor inhibitory control over gambling behaviors [16].

However, limitations inherent in cross-sectional and retrospective designs of these studies (e.g., potential biases in recall and disentangling temporal relationships), do not allow causal statements. Additionally, prior retrospective studies afford limited generalizability to the general population as they have focused primarily on people who either self-identified as a problem or pathological gambler or were in treatment for gambling problems. In contrast, prospective investigations of community-based individuals provide more conclusive evidence for the link between early impulsivity and later problem gambling. A meta-analysis of 15 longitudinal studies found a small effect for impulsivity with no statistically meaningful evidence of publication bias [17]. However, it is noteworthy that to date only four studies (some published in multiple manuscripts) measured some manifestation of impulsivity among youth younger than 18 who were then followed past age 18 [1, 14, 18–20]. Among a sample of low SES male Canadian adolescents and a representative sample of all Quebec students attending francophone schools, a constellation of impulsive, antisocial, and aggressive behaviors at age 12 predicted onset of gambling behaviors by age 23 [14]. Among disadvantaged Canadian adolescents (n = 168) who were identified by their teachers as physically aggressive and to exhibit anxiety-related behaviors, found that impulsivity at ages 12-14 predicted problem gambling approximately 4 years later independently of demographic factors and gambling behaviors at baseline [18, 19]. Another study, conducted among overlapping groups of adolescents (n = 699 and n = 625) recruited from a representative sample of households in metropolitan Buffalo, NY, found an association between impulsivity at ages 16-19 and frequency of gambling behaviors approximately 2 years later. This association was independent of socio-demographic factors, personality factors, history of substance use, extent of parental monitoring and peer delinquency [20]. It remains however that these studies did not assess impulsivity during childhood, nor did they follow participants beyond early adulthood (age 23). Furthermore, three of these samples were comprised of adolescents who were selected either because they demonstrated behavioral problems [20] or resided in disadvantaged neighborhoods [18, 20]. To date, our original investigation [1] remains the only study to measure impulsive behavior prospectively in childhood and follow participants for an average of 30 years through the peak period of onset for serious gambling problems [21, 22].

In this chapter we present this update on our original manuscript plus an examination of gender differences. In addition, we examine the specificity of the observed association between impulsive behaviors and problem gambling by conducting parallel analyses examining the link between childhood shy/depressed behaviors and problem gambling.

METHODS

Study Design, Setting and Participants

Participants were offspring of pregnant women enrolled in the New England cohorts (Boston, Massachusetts and Providence, Rhode Island) of the Collaborative Perinatal Project (CPP) between 1959 and 1966 (Figure 1) [23, 24]. The original aims of the CPP were to identify the developmental consequences of conditions arising during pregnancy and delivery. Pregnant women were enrolled and their offspring were followed periodically through age 7. During this initial phase of the CPP prospective assessments of childhood impulsive and shy/depressed behavior at age 7 were obtained.

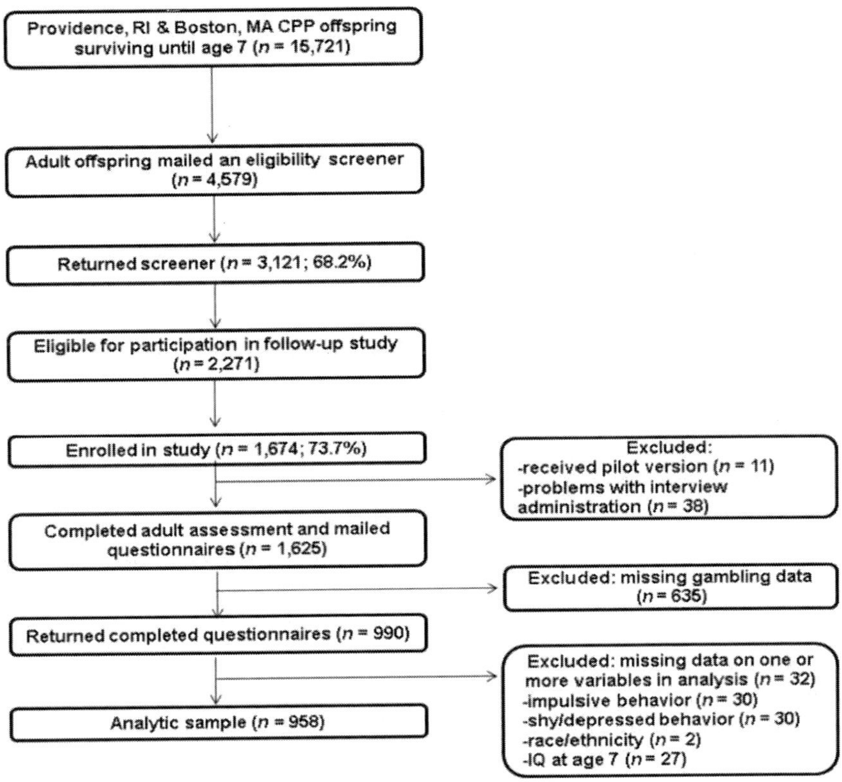

Figure 1. Flow chart of study sampling.

Building on the CPP, the Transdisciplinary Tobacco Use Research Center: New England Family Study (TTURC: NEFS) was established in 1999 to locate and interview a subsample of the adult CPP offspring in the Providence and Boston sites [25]. Participants were selected for the TTURC: NEFS study using a multi-stage sampling procedure that oversampled families in which multiple siblings participated. Screening questionnaires were mailed to 4,579 of the 15,721 offspring known to be alive at age 7. Of the 3,121 questionnaires returned (68.2%), 2,271 were eligible for participation. In total, 1,674 participants were enrolled (73.7% of eligible offspring). Data from 49 individuals were excluded because either a pilot version of the survey was administered (n = 11) or due to problems that occurred with interview administration (n = 38). This yielded 1,625 complete adult assessments. A mailing containing self-reported instruments, including the South Oaks Gambling Screen (SOGS), was sent to these 1,625 respondents and 990 participants completed and returned the SOGS. In this manuscript we report on 958 participants with data on all covariates considered in the current analyses.

The analytic sample did not differ from members of the full TTURC: NEFS sample who were excluded from these analyses on childhood impulsive ($\chi^2 = 0.005$, $df = 1$, $P = 0.94$) or shy/depressed behavior ($\chi^2 = 0.01$, $df = 1$, $P = 0.92$). The study received human subject protections approval from The Brown University and The Miriam Hospital institutional review boards. Written informed consent was obtained from participants during the adult follow-up interview after a thorough description of the study was provided.

Measures

Childhood Impulsive and Shy/Depressed Behavior

Behavioral functioning was assessed by psychologists on a structured profile completed as part of a two-hour battery of cognitive, sensory, and motor tests at the age 7 child assessment. This profile included 15 items scored on a 5-point Likert scale, with the mid-point reflecting normal or adaptive behavior. For example, response options for the emotional reactivity item ranged from '1 = extremely flat, no change in facial expressions' to '2 = somewhat flat, little change in emotional tone' to '3 = normal responsiveness, affect appropriate to situation' to '4 = mood more variable than average' to '5 = extreme instability of emotional responses, marked emotional instability'. Each item captures two different types of behavioral dysfunction; in this example flat affect versus unstable emotional reactivity. Given this, each continuous rating was converted into two new indices of problem behavior, consistent with the orientation of behavior problem checklists like the Child Behavior Checklist (CBCL) [26]. For example, two new variables were created from the original item regarding emotional reactivity: flat affect and unstable emotional reactivity. The new flat affect variable was coded as '2 = extreme flat affect' if the original item was scored a '1', '1 = some flat affect' if the original item was scored a '2', and '0 = no flat affect' if the original variable was coded a '3', '4', or '5'. The new unstable emotional reactivity variable was coded as '2 = extreme unstable emotional reactivity' if the original item was coded '5', '1 = some unstable emotional reactivity' if the original item was coded '4', and '0 = no unstable emotional reactivity' if the original item was scored as '1', '2', or '3'. This logic was used to convert the 15 continuous age 7 behavior ratings to 30 behavior problem items, with 15 of these items representing the "low" end of the original variable (e.g., flat affect) and 15 representing the "high" end of the original variable (e.g., unstable emotional reactivity). A factor analysis of these 30 derived variables yielded three behavioral subscales: impulsive,[1] shy/depressed, and outgoing. (The outgoing scale is not relevant to the current analyses and will not be discussed further.)

The resulting impulsive behavior scale was created by summing the six items found to load onto this construct in the factor analysis: unstable emotional reactivity, resistive, assertive, low frustration tolerance, impulsive, and hostile. Each of these items is associated with a form of impulsive behavior, either lack of emotional or behavioral control. Unstable emotional reactivity and low frustration tolerance are behaviors characterizing children who become emotionally reactive very quickly. Being resistive, assertive, impulsive, and hostile are behavioral descriptors of children who have difficulty sitting still, following directions, and working together with the examiner to complete the task in a timely manner. These behaviors represent the involuntary, under controlled nature of impulsivity in children [27]. Cronbach's alpha, a measure of internal

---

1 In previous publications we describe the six items reflecting impulsive behavior as "conduct problems". We view both terms as appropriate to describe the constellation of items included in this scale.

consistency, was 0.72 for the scale. Scores ranged from 0-8 (mean = 0.1, standard deviation [*SD*] = 0.6).

The shy/depressed scale was created by summing six items: shy/withdrawn, flat affect, having little to no communication, having low activity, being passive, and being fearful or apprehensive. Cronbach's alpha was 0.83 for the scale and scores ranged from 0-11 (mean = 1.2, *SD* = 1.8).

Because the distributions for the two scales were skewed (especially for the impulsive behavior scale), we created dichotomous indicators for both impulsive and shy/depressed behavior. Since only a small percentage of the sample (7.9%) was rated as exhibiting one or more impulsive behaviors we created a binary indicator based on the presence or absence of any of these problematic behaviors. We created a comparable dichotomous measure of shy/depressed behavior by categorizing those in the top decile (i.e., scores of ≥ 5 vs. scores of 1-4) as having this type of behavior problem (7.5% of the sample).

Gambling Behavior

Lifetime gambling behavior was assessed with the SOGS [28]. Designed to identify pathological gamblers, the SOGS is based on the Diagnostic and Statistical Manual of Mental Disorders, version III [29] criteria for pathologic gambling and consists of 20 items reflecting symptoms associated with pathologic gambling. The total number of endorsed items are summed and participants can be categorized as follows: 0-2 indicates non-problem gambling behavior, 3-4 indicates problem gambling, ≥ 5 indicates probable pathological gambling [28]. For the current study, we compared those with no gambling problems (i.e., those with SOGS scores ranging from 0-2) with the group of participants who evidenced at least some problems with gambling (i.e., those with a score of ≥ 3). We did not examine those with probable pathological gambling separately from problem gamblers since only a small percentage of the sample (*n* = 35, 3.7%) had SOGS scores ≥ 5.

Covariates

In addition to controlling for study site (Boston vs. Providence), we adjusted for the following demographic covariates of problem gambling identified from the literature: age (in years), gender (male vs. female), race/ethnicity, marital status, and educational attainment [30–34]. Due to a low prevalence of non-Black minorities race/ethnicity was dichotomized as Black/Hispanic/Other versus non-Hispanic White. Participants' marital status was categorized as never married, widowed/ separated/divorced, or married. Four categories of educational attainment were used: less than a high school education or GED, high school graduate, technical school or some college, or a 4 year college degree or higher. Since lower IQ appears to predict risk of impulsive behaviors [35] we also controlled for this covariate in our models. Full scale IQ scores during childhood were derived using an abbreviated version of the Wechsler Intelligence Scales for Children [36] that was administered by trained psychologists when the children were age 7. Additional variables, such as childhood socioeconomic status and mother's religion, were initially considered but dropped from the final analyses since they were not found to be associated with problem gambling. Correlates of problem gambling which could be a consequence of impulsive behavior, such as substance use and mental disorders, were considered to be on the causal pathway linking impulsive behavior and problem gambling. Consequently, these variables were not included in the regression models. Due to the relatively low prevalence of problem gambling in our sample (6.0%) we were interested in creating a parsimonious model for problem gambling.

Statistical Analysis

Two multivariable logistic models were constructed to investigate the relationship between two childhood behavior problems (impulsive and shy/depressed behavior) and problem gambling. In the first model, the dichotomous age 7 impulsive behavior variable was included as a covariate along with the demographic factors, childhood IQ, and an indicator for study site. The second model included the age 7 indicator of shy/depressed behavior in addition to the control variables.

We also tested for gender-by-behavior problem interactions for problem gambling by entering a product term between these two factors into a model that also included the main effect terms for gender and the given behavior problem (either impulsive or shy/depressed behavior) as well the control variables. Chi-square tests were used to evaluate the significance of the gender-by-behavior problem interactions. No significant interactions were found for impulsive behavior (χ^2 for interaction term = 1.37, $df = 1$, $P = 0.24$) and shy/depressed behavior (χ^2 for interaction term = 0.06, $df = 1$, $P = 0.81$). Adjusted odds ratios (AORs) and 95% confidence intervals (CIs) were computed and presented. The correlation between observations caused by the oversampling of siblings in the adult follow-up study was modeled using an exchangeable working correlation matrix and empirical standard errors were used in statistical tests. All analyses were conducted using SAS version 9 (SAS Institute, 2007).

RESULTS

Sample Characteristics

Table 1 shows the distribution of the behavioral and demographic variables for the overall analytic sample and by the problem gambling groups. Psychologist-rated impulsive behaviors were substantially more common among the group with lifetime history of problem gambling versus those without such history (24.1% vs. 6.9%). Shy-depressed behavior was also more common among participants rated as having problems with gambling (13.8% vs. 7.1%). As compared to non-problem gamblers, problem gamblers were more likely to be male (53.5% versus 34.7%), and to have never been married (41.4% versus 21.6%), and to have less than a high school education or a GED (27.6% vs. 9.3%).

Table 1. Characteristics for overall analytic sample and by lifetime problem gambling groups

Characteristic	Total (n = 958) n (%) or mean (SD)	Lifetime problem gambling[a]	
		No (n = 900) n (%) or mean (SD)	Yes (n = 58) n (%) or mean (SD)
Behavior problem at age 7			
Impulsive	76 (7.9%)	62 (6.9%)	14 (24.1%)
Shy/depressed	72 (7.5%)	64 (7.1%)	8 (13.8%)
Study site			
Boston	535 (55.8%)	513 (56.9%)	22 (37.9%)
Providence	423 (44.2%)	387 (43.1%)	36 (62.1%)
Age at adult interview	39.2 (1.8)	39.3 (1.8)	38.9 (1.7)
Male gender	343 (35.8%)	312 (34.7%)	31 (53.5%)
Race/ethnicity			
Black/Hispanic/Other	136 (14.2%)	126 (14.0%)	10 (17.2%)
Non-Hispanic White	822 (85.8%)	774 (86.0%)	48 (82.8%)
Marital status			
Never married	218 (22.8%)	194 (21.6%)	24 (41.4%)
Widowed/sep/divorced	158 (16.5%)	146 (16.2%)	12 (20.7%)
Married	582 (60.7%)	560 (62.2%)	22 (37.9%)
Educational attainment			
< High school/GED	100 (10.4%)	84 (9.3%)	16 (27.6%)
High school diploma	146 (15.2%)	140 (15.6%)	6 (10.3%)
Tech school/some college	427 (44.6%)	398 (44.2%)	29 (50.0%)
≥ 4-year college degree	285 (29.8%)	278 (30.9%)	7 (12.1%)
IQ at age 7	102.9 (12.7)	103.2 (12.6)	98.6 (13.0)

[a] Participants were classified as having problem gambling if they endorsed three or more items on the South Oaks Gambling Screen.

Multivariable Analyses

Results from the multivariable models provide evidence that the influence of early behavior problems on the development of problem gambling is specific to measures of childhood impulsivity. In our first multivariable model (Table 2, Model 1), we found a significant relationship between childhood impulsive behavior and problem gambling in adulthood after adjusting for study site, demographic factors, and childhood IQ.

Participants rated as impulsive at age 7 were over three times as likely to later develop problems with gambling (AOR: 3.24, 95% CI: 1.47-7.14). Alternatively, in our second multivariable model, we did not find a significant association between early shy/depressed behavior and later problem gambling after accounting for several potential confounders (AOR: 2.30, 95% CI: 0.97-5.44) (Table 2, Model 2).

Table 2. Adjusted associations between age 7 behavior problems and lifetime problem gambling (*n* = 958)

	Adjusted odds ratios (95% confidence intervals) for lifetime problem gambling[a]	
Characteristic	**Model 1[b]**	**Model 2[c]**
Behavior problem at age 7		
Impulsive	3.24 (1.47 - 7.14)	
Shy/depressed		2.30 (0.97 - 5.44)
Study site		
Boston (vs. Providence)	0.68 (0.33 - 1.41)	0.72 (0.35 - 1.48)
Age at adult interview	0.96 (0.81 - 1.14)	0.93 (0.79 - 1.10)
Male gender	2.00 (1.12 - 3.56)	2.25 (1.28 - 3.95)
Race/ethnicity		
Black/Hispanic/Other (vs. Non-Hispanic White)	0.71 (0.33 - 1.55)	0.80 (0.38 - 1.68)
Marital status		
Never married	Reference	Reference
Widowed/sep/divorced	0.66 (0.29 - 1.48)	0.67 (0.30 - 1.47)
Married	0.42 (0.22 - 0.79)	0.41 (0.22 - 0.76)
Educational attainment		
<High school/GED	Reference	Reference
High school diploma	0.34 (0.12 - 1.03)	0.31 (0.10 - 0.94)
Tech school/some college	0.65 (0.29 - 1.47)	0.58 (0.26 - 1.27)
≥4-year college degree	0.24 (0.08 - 0.78)	0.22 (0.07 - 0.68)
IQ at age 7[d]	0.99 (0.66 - 1.48)	1.05 (0.69 - 1.60)

[a] Participants were classified as having problem gambling if they endorsed three or more items on the South Oaks Gambling Screen.

[b] Adjusted model for the association between impulsive behavior at age 7 and lifetime problem gambling.

[c] Adjusted model for the association between shy/depressed behavior at age 7 and lifetime problem gambling.

[d] Adjusted odds ratios are expressed for a one standard deviation change (15 points) in IQ scores.

Our conclusions regarding the specificity of the link between impulsivity and later problem gambling are bolstered by findings from additional multivariable models (data not shown) that were conducted in order to examine whether our selected cut-point for the shy/depressed scale may have accounted for our lack of significant findings (only 8 participants with scores of ≥ 5 on the age 7 shy/depressed behavior scale became problem gamblers). We found that models using less stringent thresholds for categorizing participants as shy/depressed (e.g., any shy/depressed behavior, ≥ 3 shy/depressed behaviors) led to the same conclusion that childhood shy/depressed behavior does not independently increase the risk of problem gambling by adulthood.

Our findings also implicate the independent role of demographic factors in the etiology of problem gambling. More specifically, in the adjusted models we found that males experienced a significant, approximately two-fold increased risk of problem gambling as compared to females. Alternatively, being married (versus being never married) and having a college-level education (versus less than high school or GED) had a significant protective effect.

CONCLUSION

To date, this is the only prospective investigation of the link between childhood impulsive behavior and life-time risk of problem gambling assessed at mid-adulthood. In line with previous works, we found that men are more likely than women to be problem gamblers, and that being married and relatively more educated protects against development of problem gambling [6, 30, 37–41]. Our key findings were two-fold. First, we found that 7-year old children exhibiting impulsive behaviors had an elevated risk of becoming problem gamblers during their lifetime. Secondly, we found that shy/depressed behavior at age 7 does not confer an elevated risk of problem gambling by mid-adulthood, a finding that was recently replicated in another prospective population based study [14]. Furthermore, failure to find a significant association between shy/depressed behavior and problem gambling was not likely due to our selected cut-point for the shy/depressed scale. Together these findings highlight the specificity of the association between impulsive behaviors and problem gambling.

Impulsivity and impulse control disorders tend to impair individuals' ability to resist behaviors that can be harmful to the person or to others. The link between behavioral manifestations of impulsivity and lifetime risk of problem gambling suggest an early pathway to gambling problems. This information can help further refine existing therapies of differing modalities, including pharmacotherapy, psychosocial treatment, and cognitive behavioral therapies, for treatment of problem gambling [43, 44].

However, we must note that programs for preventing gambling onset among children and youth are of limited utility [45, 46]. Furthermore, although non-impulsive children are at a relatively lower risk of becoming problem gamblers than impulsive children their far larger numbers gives rise to more cases of problem gambling (in our sample, 76% of problem gamblers did not exhibit impulsive behaviors at age 7), suggests that universal public health efforts promoting the health and well-being of all children are likely a more efficient approach to preventing a host of negative outcomes associated with early impulsivity [47]. The premise of this approach is that even individuals not at risk of the target condition benefit from improved functioning, and by promoting psychological wellbeing of all individuals this approach avoids issues associated with labeling individuals as having psychopathology [48]. Finally, decisions regarding timing and place of delivery of such services should consider that the onset of gambling behavior appears to be influenced by both a propensity towards impulsivity and having low socio-economic status [49].

Our findings should be considered in light of this study's limitations and strengths. Impulsivity is a complex behavioral characteristic to measure. For example, it could reflect an inability to inhibit a thought or an inability to inhibit a behavior, such as gambling [50]. Behaviors representing an involuntary lack of control over behavior (i.e., uncooperative with the examiner, hostile, assertive, and impulsive) [27] or emotional regulation (i.e., low frustration tolerance and unstable emotional reactivity) are indicators of an impulsive child. Our data do not assess cognitive components of impulsivity. Moreover, our behavioral ratings were made by psychologists as part of a 2 hour cognitive and behavioral assessment and, as such, reflect child behavior exhibited over a short interval in a limited setting. These ratings likely capture only the most seriously impulsive youth who were unable to modify their behavior during the structured assessment. It is therefore likely that many children with lower levels of impulsive behavior were misclassified as non-impulsive, perhaps resulting in an underestimate of the true association between impulsivity and problem gambling. Additionally, as the lifetime version of SOGS was used, reported gambling problems may not have occurred at the same time. Lastly, the adult participants included in the TTURC: NEFS follow-up study cannot be considered representative of the full CPP cohort. Participants were selected on the basis of inclusion criteria that were necessary for the major sub-studies conducted with the follow-up sample but not for the analyses described in this chapter. Finally, results of our examination of gender-by-behavior problem interactions should be viewed with caution due to our low statistical power to test for interactions and in light of recent evidence of gender differences in risks for problem gambling among adults [51, 52].

Several strengths of the study are also noteworthy. Despite possible limitations with our measure of impulsive behavior, our assessments were collected prospectively in childhood, unlike in most prior studies. Use of the SOGS, a widely used valid measure of problem gambling, is another strength of this study. Our sensitivity analysis provided evidence that impulsivity is a particular type of childhood problem associated with an elevated likelihood of subsequent problem gambling. Additionally, to date, this is the only study to predict problem gambling over the span of 30-years among a non-referred sample, reflecting the generalizability of our findings to a more broad population than most prior work.

REFERENCES

[1] Shenassa, ED; Paradis, AD; Dolan, SL; Wilhelm, CS; Buka, SL. Childhood impulsive behavior and problem gambling by adulthood: a

30-year prospective community-based study. *Addiction.*, 2012, 107(1), 160-168. doi:10.1111/j.1360-0443.2011.03571.x.

[2] Hodgins, DC; Petry, NM. The world of gambling: the National Gambling Experiences series. *Addiction.*, 2016, 111(9), 1516-1518. doi: 10.1111/add.13445.

[3] Nautiyal, KM; Okuda, M; Hen, R; Blanco, C. Gambling disorder: an integrative review of animal and human studies. *Ann N Y Acad Sci.*, 2017, 1394(1), 106-127. doi: 10.1111/nyas.13356.

[4] Shaffer, HJ; Korn, DA. Gambling and related mental disorders: a public health analysis. *Annu Rev Public Health.*, 2002, 23, 171-212. doi: 10.1146/annurev.publhealth.23.100901.140532.

[5] Welte, JW; Barnes, GM; Wieczorek, WF; Tidwell, MC; Parker, J. Gambling participation in the U.S.--results from a national survey. *J Gambl Stud.*, 2002, 18(4), 313-337. http://www.ncbi.nlm.nih.gov/pubmed/12514913.

[6] Gerstein, D.R. et al., 1999. *Gambling Impact and Behavior Study*: National Opinion Research Center. Chicago, IL: NORC; 1999.

[7] Goudriaan, AE; Yücel, M; van Holst, RJ. Getting a grip on problem gambling: what can neuroscience tell us? *Front Behav Neurosci.*, 2014, 8(141). doi: 10.3389/fnbeh.2014.00141.

[8] Janiri, L; Martinotti, G; Dario, T; Schifano, F; Bria, P. The Gamblers' Temperament and Character Inventory (TCI) personality profile. *Subst Use Misuse.*, 2007, 42(6), 975-984. doi: 10.1080/10826080701202445.

[9] Langenbucher, J; Bavly, L; Labouvie, E; Sanjuan, PM; Martin, CS. Clinical features of pathological gambling in an addictions treatment cohort. *Psychol Addict Behav.*, 2001, 15(1), 77-79. http://www.ncbi.nlm.nih.gov/pubmed/11255942.

[10] Specker, SM; Carlson, GA; Christenson, GA; Marcotte, M. Impulse control disorders and attention deficit disorder in pathological gamblers. *Ann Clin Psychiatry.*, 1995, 7(4), 175-179. http://www.ncbi.nlm.nih.gov/pubmed/8721891.

[11] Alessi, SM; Petry, NM. Pathological gambling severity is associated with impulsivity in a delay discounting procedure. *Behav Processes.*,

2003, 64(3), 345-354. http://www.ncbi.nlm.nih.gov/pubmed/14580703.

[12] Hodgins, DC; Holub, A. Components of Impulsivity in Gambling Disorder. *Int J Ment Health Addict.*, 13(6), 699-711. doi:10.1007/s11469-015-9572-z.

[13] MacKillop, J; Miller, JD; Fortune, E; et al. Multidimensional examination of impulsivity in relation to disordered gambling. *Exp Clin Psychopharmacol.*, 2014, 22(2), 176-185. doi: 10.1037/a0035874.

[14] Allami, Y; Vitaro, F; Brendgen, M; Carbonneau, R; Tremblay, RE. Identifying at-risk profiles and protective factors for problem gambling: a longitudinal study across adolescence and early adulthood. *Psychol Addict Behav.*, 2018. doi: 10.1037/ adb0000356.

[15] Maclaren, VV; Fugelsang, JA; Harrigan, KA; Dixon, MJ. The personality of pathological gamblers: a meta-analysis. *Clin Psychol Rev.*, 2011, 31(6), 1057-1067. doi: 10.1016/j.cpr.2011.02.002.

[16] Chowdhury, NS; Livesey, EJ; Blaszczynski, A; Harris, JA. Pathological gambling and motor impulsivity: a systematic review with meta-analysis. *J Gambl Stud.*, 2017, 33(4), 1213-1239. doi: 10.1007/s10899-017-9683-5.

[17] Dowling, NA; Merkouris, SS; Greenwood, CJ; Oldenhof, E; Toumbourou, JW; Youssef, GJ. Early risk and protective factors for problem gambling: a systematic review and meta-analysis of longitudinal studies. *Clin Psychol Rev.*, 2017, 51, 109-124. doi: 10.1016/j.cpr.2016.10.008.

[18] Vitaro, F; Arseneault, L; Tremblay, RE. Impulsivity predicts problem gambling in low SES adolescent males. *Addiction.*, 1999, 94(4), 565-575. doi: 10.1046/j.1360-0443.1999.94456511.x.

[19] Vitaro, F; Brendgen, M; Ladouceur, R; Tremblay, RE. Gambling, delinquency, and drug use during adolescence: mutual influences and common risk factors. *J Gambl Stud.*, 2001, 17(3), 171-190. http://www.ncbi.nlm.nih.gov/pubmed/11761603.

[20] Barnes, GM; Welte, JW; Hoffman, JH; Dintcheff, BA. Gambling and alcohol use among youth: influences of demographic, socialization,

and individual factors. *Addict Behav.*, 1999, 24(6), 749-767. http://www. ncbi.nlm.nih.gov/pubmed/10628510.

[21] Bland, RC; Newman, SC; Orn, H; Stebelsky, G. Epidemiology of pathological gambling in Edmonton. *Can J Psychiatry.*, 1993, 38(2), 108-112. http://www.ncbi.nlm.nih.gov/pubmed/8467435.

[22] Verdura Vizcaíno, EJ; Fernández-Navarro, P; Petry, N; Rubio, G; Blanco, C. Differences between early-onset pathological gambling and later-onset pathological gambling: data from the National Epidemiologic Survey on Alcohol and Related Conditions (NESARC). *Addiction.*, 2014, 109(5), 807-813. http://www.ncbi.nlm.nih.gov/pubmed/25006638.

[23] Broman, SH. The Collaborative Perinatal Project: an overview. In: Mednick S, Harway M, Finello K, eds. *Handbook of Longitudinal Research.* New York, NY: Praeger, 1984, 185-215.

[24] Niswander, KR; Gordon, M. *The Women and Their Pregnancies: The Collaborative Perinatal Study of the National Institute of Neurological Diseases and Stroke.* Washington, DC: US Government Print Office, 1972.

[25] Shenassa, ED; Papandonatos, GD; Rogers, ML; Buka, SL. Elevated risk of nicotine dependence among sib-pairs discordant for maternal smoking during pregnancy: evidence from a 40-year longitudinal study. *Epidemiology.*, 2015, 26(3), 441-447. doi: 10.1097/EDE.0000000000000270.

[26] Achenbach, TM. *Manual for the Child Behavior Checklist/2-3 and 1992 Profile.* Burlington, VT: University of Vermont, 1991.

[27] Eisenberg, N; Spinrad, TL; Fabes, RA; et al. The relations of effortful control and impulsivity to children's resiliency and adjustment. *Child Dev.*, 2004, 75(1), 25-46. http://www.ncbi.nlm.nih.gov/pubmed/15015673.

[28] Lesieur, HR; Blume, SB. The South Oaks Gambling Screen (SOGS): a new instrument for the identification of pathological gamblers. *Am J Psychiatry.*, 1987, 144(9), 1184-1188. doi:10.1176/ajp.144.9.1184.

[29] American Psychiatric Association. *Diagnostic and Statistical Manual of Mental Disorders.* 3rd ed. Washington, DC: American Psychiatric Association, 1980.

[30] Welte, JW; Barnes, GM; Wieczorek, WF; Tidwell, MCO; Parker, JC. Risk factors for pathological gambling. *Addict Behav.*, 2004, 29(2), 323-335. http://www.ncbi.nlm.nih.gov/pubmed/14732420.

[31] Cunningham-Williams, RM; Grucza, RA; Cottler, LB; et al. Prevalence and predictors of pathological gambling: results from the St. Louis personality, health and lifestyle (SLPHL) study. *J Psychiatr Res.*, 2005, 39(4), 377-390. doi: 10.1016/j.jpsychires.2004.09.002.

[32] Petry, NM; Stinson, FS; Grant, BF. Comorbidity of DSM-IV pathological gambling and other psychiatric disorders: results from the National Epidemiologic Survey on Alcohol and Related Conditions. *J Clin Psychiatry.*, 2005, 66(5), 564-574. http:// www. ncbi.nlm. nih.gov/pubmed/15889941.

[33] Petry, NM; Kiluk, BD. Suicidal ideation and suicide attempts in treatment-seeking pathological gamblers. *J Nerv Ment Dis.*, 2002, 190(7), 462-469. doi: 10.1097/01.NMD.0000022447.27689.96.

[34] Scherrer, JF; Slutske, WS; Xian, H; et al. Factors associated with pathological gambling at 10-year follow-up in a national sample of middle-aged men. *Addiction.*, 2007, 102(6), 970-978. doi: 10.1111/ j.1360-0443.2007.01833.x.

[35] Ackerman, PL; Heggestad, ED. Intelligence, personality, and interests: evidence for overlapping traits. *Psychol Bull.*, 1997, 121(2), 219-245. http://www.ncbi.nlm.nih.gov/pubmed/9100487.

[36] Wechsler, D. *Manual for the Wechsler Preschool and Primary Scale of Intelligence.* New York: Psychological Corporation, 1963.

[37] Volberg, RA. The prevalence and demographics of pathological gamblers: implications for public health. *Am J Public Health.*, 1994, 84(2), 237-241. http://www.ncbi.nlm.nih.gov/pubmed/8296947.

[38] Afifi, TO; Cox, BJ; Martens, PJ; Sareen, J; Enns, MW. Demographic and social variables associated with problem gambling among men and women in Canada. *Psychiatry Res.*, 2010, 178(2), 395-400. doi: 10.1016/j.psychres.2009.10.003.

[39] Fröberg, F; Modin, B; Rosendahl, IK; Tengström, A; Hallqvist, J. The association between compulsory school achievement and problem gambling among Swedish young people. *J Adolesc Health.*, 2015, 56(4), 420-428. doi: 10.1016/ j.jadohealth.2014.12.007.

[40] Delfabbro, P; King, D; Griffiths, MD. From adolescent to adult gambling: an analysis of longitudinal gambling patterns in South Australia. *J Gambl Stud.*, 2014, 30(3), 547-563. doi: 10.1007/s10899-013-9384-7.

[41] Edgerton, JD; Melnyk, TS; Roberts, LW. Problem gambling and the youth-to-adulthood transition: assessing problem gambling severity trajectories in a sample of young adults. *J Gambl Stud.*, 2014, 30(3), 1-23.

[42] Blanco, C; Hanania, J; Petry, NM; et al. Towards a comprehensive developmental model of pathological gambling. *Addiction.*, 2015, 110(8), 1340-1351. doi:10.1111/add.12946.

[43] Choi, SW; Shin, YC; Kim, DJ; et al. Treatment modalities for patients with gambling disorder. *Ann Gen Psychiatry.*, 2017, 16(1), 23. doi: 10.1186/s12991-017-0146-2.

[44] Petry, NM. *Pathological Gambling: Etiology; Comorbidity, and Treatment.* 1st ed. Washington, DC: American Psychological Association, 2005.

[45] Dickson, LM; Derevensky, JL; Gupta, R. The prevention of gambling problems in youth: a conceptual framework. *J Gambl Stud.*, 2002, 18(2), 97-159. http://www.ncbi.nlm.nih.gov/pubmed/ 12096450.

[46] Keen, B; Blaszczynski, A; Anjoul, F. Systematic review of empirically evaluated school-based gambling education programs. *J Gambl Stud.*, 2017, 33(1), 301-325. doi:10.1007/s10899-016-9641-7.

[47] Hudziak, J; Ivanova, MY. The Vermont family based approach. *Child Adolesc Psychiatr Clin N Am.*, 2016, 25(2), 167-178. doi: 10.1016/ j.chc.2015.11.002.

[48] Cushing, CC; Brannon, EE; Suorsa, KI; Wilson, DK. Systematic review and meta-analysis of health promotion interventions for children and adolescents using an ecological framework. *J Pediatr Psychol.*, 2014, 39(8), 949-962. doi:10.1093/ jpepsy/jsu042.

[49] Auger, N; Lo, E; Cantinotti, M; O'Loughlin, J. Impulsivity and socio-economic status interact to increase the risk of gambling onset among youth. *Addiction.*, 2010, 105(12), 2176-2183. doi:10. 1111/ j.1360-0443.2010.03100.x.

[50] Bechara, A. Risky business: emotion, decision-making, and addiction. *J Gambl Stud.*, 2003, 19(1), 23-51. http://www.ncbi.nlm.nih.gov/pubmed/12635539.

[51] Delfabbro, P; Thomas, A; Armstrong, A. Gender differences in the presentation of observable risk indicators of problem gambling. *J Gambl Stud.*, 2018, 34(1), 119-132. doi:10.1007/s10899-017-9691-5.

[52] Farstad, SM; von Ranson, KM; Hodgins, DC; El-Guebaly, N; Casey, DM; Schopflocher, DP. The influence of impulsiveness on binge eating and problem gambling: A prospective study of gender differences in Canadian adults. *Psychol Addict Behav.*, 2015, 29(3), 805-812. doi: 10.1037/adb0000069.

In: Understanding Impulsive Behavior
Editor: Christian Braddon
ISBN: 978-1-53613-815-3

Chapter 7

THE INFLUENCE OF DEMOGRAPHIC FEATURES, SUBSTANCE USE AND PSYCHIATRIC DISORDERS IN THE OVERT MANIFESTATION OF IMPULSIVITY: DOES GENDER MATTER?

Carlos Alfonso Tovilla-Zárate[1], Rebeca Robles-García[2,*], Ana Fresán[3,†], Thelma Beatriz González-Castro[4], Yazmín Hernández-Díaz[4], Lilia López-Narváez[4] and Isela E. Juárez-Rojop[5]

[1]Universidad Juárez Autónoma de Tabasco, División Académica Multidisciplinaria de Comalcalco, Comalcalco, Tabasco, México

[2]Dirección de Investigaciones Epidemiológicas, y Sociales, Instituto Nacional de Psiquiatría Ramón de la Fuente Muñiz, Ciudad de México, México

---

* Corresponding Author Email: Rebeca Robles-García PsyD, PhD. Dirección de Investigaciones Epidemiológicas y Sociales. Email: reberobles@hotmail.com.

† Corresponding Author Email: Ana Fresan, PsyD, PhD. Subdirección de Investigaciones Clínicas. Email: fresan@imp.edu.mx.

[3]Subdirección de Investigaciones Clínicas, Instituto Nacional de Psiquiatría Ramón de la Fuente Muñiz, Ciudad de México, México
[4]Universidad Juárez Autónoma de Tabasco, División Académica Multidisciplinaria de Jalpa de Méndez, Jalpa de Méndez, Tabasco, México
[5]Hospital General de Yajalón. Secretaría de Salud, Yajalón, Chiapas, México

ABSTRACT

Introduction: Impulsivity is defined as a predisposition toward unplanned reactions to stimuli. Its association with psychiatric disorders is not new since it has been considered a common clinical feature in several psychiatric diagnoses and a major predictor of substance use and attempted suicide.

The construct of impulsivity encompasses various components, including personality, cognition and behavior and manifests differently across psychiatric disorders. One can therefore assume that there is not only an exclusive, one-way direction in the association between psychiatric disorders and impulsivity as the latter may influence the way impulsivity manifests. In addition, other variables such as gender and substance may also have a direct impact or act as moderators of impulsivity traits.

Although evidence of the association between impulsivity, psychiatric disorders, substance abuse and certain individual characteristics such as gender exists, it remains unclear whether they contribute to increasing impulsivity traits, and whether this influence differs between men and women.

Objective: To determine the impact of demographic variables and substance use in the overt expression of impulsivity in men and women with and without mental disorders.

Method: A total of 318 psychiatric patients from the outpatient services of two institutions and 184 healthy subjects were recruited. Patients were included if they were ≥18 years of age, met DSM-IV criteria for a psychotic, mood- or stress-related disorder and were clinically stable enough according to the treating physician to complete the study assessments. Healthy subjects were screened using the Structured Clinical

Interview for DSM-IV (SCID-I) and were excluded if any diagnostic criteria was met or if they verbally reported a history of psychiatric disorders.

Demographic data and comorbidity with substance use were obtained from the patients' medical records and a direct clinical interview with all the respondents. Current use of alcohol, nicotine, cannabis and cocaine was recorded through a closed-ended (yes/no) question. Plutchik's Impulsivity Scale was used to assess impulsivity.

Results: A higher frequency of patients reported alcohol (40.4% vs. 29.3%, $p = 0.01$), cannabis (16.4% vs. 2.2%, $p < 0.001$), cocaine (9.3% vs. 1.1%, $p < 0.001$) and nicotine (29.6% vs. 8.7%) use in comparison with healthy subjects. They were also more impulsive than healthy controls (22.5, S.D. = 7.5 vs. 13.7, S.D. = 6.6; $p < 0.001$) while women in the group of patients were more impulsive than men (23.5, S.D. = 7.4 vs. 20.1, S.D. = 7.1, $p = 0.002$).

The presence of a psychiatric disorder and being younger were variables related to impulsivity in both men and women. However, other significant related variables were different by gender. In men, these variables were cocaine use, unemployment and being married; whereas in women they included alcohol use and lower educational attainment

Conclusions: Impulsivity is present in patients with psychiatric disorders and the differences observed between them and healthy subjects can be at least partly explained by the younger age and correspondingly lower educational attainment reported in the clinical sample. In patients with psychiatric disorders, its manifestation may vary according to gender. According to various studies, this difference can be explained by the effects of hormones, but also by the different manifestation of impairments in cognitive performance and emotional regulation found between men and women.

Our results for the association between substance use and impulsivity are consistent with previous research. However, our findings highlight the way substance use has a different impact on impulsivity features by gender since frequency of use and motivations for use may differ between them.

Despite its various limitations, our study emphasizes the importance of the assessment of impulsivity in everyday clinical practice and the need for intervention strategies designed to reduce or manage its presence in a proactive way.

Keywords: impulsivity, mental disorders, gender, substance use

1. Introduction

Impulsivity has been defined as a predisposition toward rapid, unplanned reactions to internal or external stimuli, with diminished regard for the negative consequences of these reactions for the impulsive individual or others (Moeller et al. 2001). There are several theoretical constructs designed to explain impulsivity (Miller et al. 2003), including poor planning for the future and certain specific personality features such as high novelty seeking (Cloninger et al. 1991; Plutchik and Van Praag 1989), for instance. It has been even suggested that impulsivity is at the interface between thoughts and actions (Klonsky and May 2010).

The association between impulsivity and psychiatric disorders is by no means new. It is considered a common feature in various psychiatric disorders including bipolar disorder, schizophrenia, borderline personality disorder and substance addictions (Mitchell and Potenza 2014; Watkins and Meyer 2013). It has also emerged as a clinical predictor of suicide attempts in patients with affective disorders and schizophrenia (Chachamovich et al. 2009; Iancu et al. 2010; Iancu et al. 2006; Swann et al. 2005). This association can be explained by the presence of hopelessness regarding the future and the way impulsivity interferes in the patient's decision-making process, eventually expressed as external or self-directed aggression (Moeller et al. 2001; Spivak et al. 2003).

Although most studies have described the contribution of impulsivity to the development and expression of a psychiatric disorder (Bauer et al. 2015; Galvez et al. 2014; Ortal et al. 2015), little has been written in terms of the influence of a psychiatric disorder on the overt manifestation of impulsivity. The construct of impulsivity encompasses personality traits, cognitive and behavioral components, and involves both normal and abnormal individual differences regarding the degree and severity of related consequences (Sharma et al. 2014). Moreover, some authors have noted that, at the clinical level, impulsivity manifests itself differently across disorders (Congdon and Canli 2005; Hodgins and Holub 2015). Impulsivity associated with depression is different from impulsivity associated with borderline personality disorder or schizophrenia, for example. Thus, we cannot assume an exclusively one-way direction in the association between the two phenomena since psychiatric disorders can affect the way impulsivity manifests itself in a person.

A similar debate about the relation between substance use and impulsivity exists. Some studies regard impulsivity as a stable trait irrespective of substance use (Dom et al. 2006; Farley and Kim-Spoon 2015), whereas others have posited that the relation between impulsivity and drug use is bidirectional (Bickel and Yi 2006). Although the general consensus is that higher impulsivity leads to engagement in substance use, with most research studies focusing on this, research examining the effects of substance use on impulsivity is scarce and further research is needed.

Moreover, impulsivity can also show variations according to individual characteristics as well as environmental variables, (d'Acremont and Van der Linden 2005; Hipwell et al. 2010; Wrege et al. 2014) including gender. Several biological, cognitive, behavioral and social studies suggest that men are typically more impulsive than women (Erez et al. 2014). These results have been supported by meta-analytic data showing that men score higher than women on specific aspects of impulsivity (Eysenck et al. 1985). Likewise, lower novelty seeking has frequently been associated with less impulsive behavior in women aged 26-59 (Fresan et al. 2011; Witte et al. 2012). However, for certain specific behaviors such as suicidal and non-suicidal self-injury, women are reported to be more impulsive than men (Zhang and Lin 2014). Gender may therefore moderate associations between impulsivity and some risk behaviors, with stronger associations being observed in men than women in specific circumstances (Stoltenberg et al. 2008).

In short, although evidence of the association between impulsivity, psychiatric disorders, substance abuse and certain individual characteristics and environmental variables exists, we lack a detailed understanding of whether the presence of a mental disorder, the use of certain substances, and/or specific demographic characteristics could contribute to increasing impulsivity traits, and of whether this influence differs between men and women. This information could contribute to developing gender-based interventions to reduce impulsivity and related risk behaviors in both the psychiatric and general population.

In this direction, the main objective of this study was to determine the impact of demographic variables and substance use in the overt expression of impulsivity in men and women with and without mental disorders.

2. METHODS

The study was conducted in accordance with Good Clinical Practices. The study protocol was approved by the Ethics and Research Review Boards of Comalcalco General Hospital and the University of Tabasco (UJAT-DAMC), Mexico; and the Ramón de la Fuente National Institute of Psychiatry (INPRF) in Mexico City, Mexico. After receiving a comprehensive explanation of the nature of the study, all the respondents granted their written informed consent to participate in the study. All the subjects took part voluntarily and were not paid for their participation.

2.1. Clinical Sample

The sample of clinical cases was consecutively recruited in the outpatient services of the INPRF and of Comalcalco General Hospital, Tabasco. We decided to include only outpatients to avoid the confusing effects of hospitalization on the everyday activities or usual behavior of patients. In both sites, patients were included if they were ≥18 years of age, met DSM-IV criteria for a psychotic, mood or stress-related disorder based on the Structured Clinical Interview for DSM-IV [SCID-I] (First et al. 1996) and were clinically stable enough according to treating physician to answer Plutchik's Impulsivity Scale. Patients with a concomitant medical or neurological illness, severe agitation, overt aggressive behavior or current substance abuse or dependence, with the exception of nicotine, were excluded.

2.2. Healthy Subjects

Subjects were recruited from the blood donor center at Comalcalco General Hospital. Males or females were included if they were ≥18 years of age and capable of consenting to participate in the study. They were screened with the SCID-I and subjects who met the criteria for any diagnosis or were suffering from any medical or neurological disease, or had any current substance abuse or dependence (except for nicotine) were excluded. Subjects were also excluded if they verbally reported a history of psychiatric disorders or previous use of a psychiatric service.

2.3. Assessments

Demographic and substance use data were obtained from patients' medical records and a direct clinical interview with all the subjects. Current use of alcohol, nicotine, cannabis and cocaine was recorded through a closed-ended (yes/no) question. Plutchik's Impulsivity Scale was used for the assessment of impulsivity. It is a self-administered questionnaire with 15 items scored on a four-point frequency scale (0–4 points), designed to measure the subject's tendency to engage in impulsive, spur-of-the-moment behaviors, which reflects possible losses of control (Plutchik and Van Praag 1989). A previous study of Mexican psychiatric patients showed that the main areas of impulsivity rated by the scale are: 1) self-control, 2) planning of future action, 3) physiological behaviors and 4) spontaneous behavior (Páez et al. 1996). The total score of impulsivity in each area scale is obtained from the sum of each item score. Higher scores are indicative of higher impulsivity. For the present study, the mean score of the scale was used to classify patients as impulsive or non-impulsive. Moreover, all subjects were instructed to complete Plutchik's Impulsivity Scale on the basis of their most common behaviors rather than isolated events during their lives.

2.4. Statistical Analysis

All analyses were performed using SPSS statistical software Version 20.0. Demographic and clinical characteristics were described with frequencies and percentages for categorical variables and means and standard deviations (S.D.) for continuous variables. The initial comparisons between patients and control subjects were analyzed using Chi-square tests (x^2) for categorical variables and with Independent Sample t Tests for continuous variables. For the comparison of impulsivity traits between patients and healthy subjects by gender, an Analysis of Variance (ANOVA) followed by Bonferroni's corrections was performed.

Two multiple linear regression models with the backward conditional method were conducted, including demographic and substance use as explanatory variables and the total impulsivity score as the outcome variable. The first model was used to determine the variables related to impulsivity in men, and the second model for those in women. β-coefficients were used as an effect size measure of the variables with the highest association with impulsivity. The significance level for tests was established at $p \leq 0.05$.

3. Results

3.1. Sample Description

One hundred and eighty-four healthy subjects and 280 psychiatric patients aged 18 to 70 were recruited. A total of 53.9% (n = 151) of the patient sample, were diagnosed with a mood disorder, followed by 23.6% (n = 66) with schizophrenia and 22.5% (n = 63) with stress-related disorders.

Table 1. Demographics, substance use and impulsivity between groups

	Healthy Subjects n=184		Psychiatric Patients n=280		Statistics
	n	%	n	%	
Gender					
Female	114	62.0	196	70.0	x^2= 3.24, p=0.07
Male	70	38.0	84	30.0	
Marital status					
Married	87	47.3	111	39.6	x^2= 2.64, p=0.10
Single	97	52.7	169	60.4	
Employment status					
Employed	73	39.7	98	35.0	x^2= 1.04, p=0.30
Unemployed	111	60.3	182	65.0	
Alcohol use					
No	130	70.7	167	59.6	x^2= 5.84, p=0.016
Yes	54	29.3	113	40.4	
Cannabis use					
No	180	97.8	234	83.6	x^2= 23.46, p<0.001
Yes	4	2.2	46	16.4	
Cocaine use					
No	182	98.9	254	90.7	x^2= 13.16, p<0.001
Yes	2	1.1	26	9.3	
Nicotine use					
No	168	91.3	197	70.4	x^2= 29.02, p<0.001
Yes	16	8.7	83	29.6	
	Mean	**SD**	**Mean**	**SD**	
Age	33.2	13.3	28.8	9.4	t= 3.8, p<0.001
Length of education (years)	12.2	4.8	10.5	3.6	t= 4.0, p<0.001
Plutchik Impulsivity Scale					
Self-control	5.2	3.5	9.4	4.0	t= -11.8, p<0.001
Planning of future action	4.8	2.8	6.2	2.2	t= -5.6, p<0.001
Physiological behaviors	1.0	1.2	2.1	1.6	t= -7.6, p<0.001
Spontaneous behavior	2.6	1.9	4.7	2.1	t= -11.1, p<0.001
Total	13.7	6.6	22.5	7.5	t= -13.1, p<0.001

3.2. Demographic Characteristics, Substance Use and Impulsivity Traits between Patients and Healthy Subjects

Significant differences emerged between the groups, with patients being younger and having lower educational attainment. Moreover, a higher proportion of patients reported substance use as well as higher impulsivity traits compared with healthy subjects (Table 1).

3.3. Impulsivity Traits by Gender in Patients and Healthy Subjects

Means and standard deviations of impulsivity traits by group and gender are shown in Table 2. For all the impulsivity dimensions, significant differences emerged among the four groups according to the ANOVA model ($p < 0.001$). Nevertheless, the post hoc tests showed no differences between men and women in the control group. In the clinical group, differences by gender were found in the *self-control, and spontaneous behavior* dimensions, as well as in the total score of Plutchik's Scale, where women scored higher than men.

Table 2. Impulsivity traits according to group and gender

Plutchik Impulsivity Scale	Healthy Subjects				Psychiatric Patients			
	Men (n=70)		Women (n=114)		Men (n=84)		Women (n=196)	
	Mean	S.D.	Mean	S.D.	Mean	S.D.	Mean	S.D.
Self-control	5.2	3.5	5.2	3.5	8.3	4.2	9.8	3.8
	p=1.00				p=0.01			
Planning of future action	4.5	2.7	4.9	2.8	5.9	2.1	6.3	2.2
	p=1.00				p=1.00			
Physiological behaviors	1.1	1.2	1.0	1.1	1.8	1.3	2.2	1.7
	p=1.00				p=0.20			
Spontaneous behavior	2.6	2.0	2.6	1.8	4.0	2.0	5.0	2.1
	p=1.00				p<0.001			
Total	13.6	7.2	13.8	6.3	20.1	7.1	23.5	7.4
	p=1.00				p=0.002			

3.4. Demographic and Substance Use Estimates of Impulsivity in Men and Women

Both linear regression models (for men and women) included demographic variables as well as substance use variables. The presence of a mental disorder was the variable most significantly related to impulsivity in both men and women. Moreover, in both models, being younger was significantly associated with a higher level of impulsivity.

Other variables were related to impulsivity yet differed between men and women. Cocaine use, being married and unemployed significantly contributed to impulsivity in men; while alcohol use and lower educational attainment were related to impulsivity in women (Table 3).

Table 3. Linear regression models for impulsivity in men and women

	Effect Size β Coefficient	Confidence Interval 95%	Significance
Men [a]			
Psychiatric illness	5.61	3.37 – 7.85	<0.001
Use of cocaine	4.63	0.99 – 8.26	0.01
Married	3.81	1.15 – 6.48	0.005
Unemployed	3.14	0.88 – 5.39	0.007
Age	-0.19	-0.30 - -0.09	<0.001
Women [b]			
Psychiatric illness	7.63	5.89 – 9.37	<0.001
Use of alcohol	3.46	1.18 – 5.74	0.003
Age	-0.11	-0.19 - -0.04	0.002
Education	-0.21	-0.40 - -0.02	0.02

[a] Goodness-of-fit, adjusted $R^2 = 0.275$.
[b] Goodness-of-fit, adjusted $R^2 = 0.362$.

4. Discussion

This study was designed to explore gender differences regarding impulsivity in psychiatric patients and healthy subjects, and to analyze possible variables that could help clinicians identify the presence of impulsivity in an individual. It did so because there are several papers hypothesizing that impulsivity results from biological as well as environmental vulnerabilities (Lundahl et al. 2015; Mancke et al. 2015).

In an initial analysis, we compared impulsivity features between a group of psychiatric patients and healthy subjects. The outcomes of Plutchik´s Scale showed that psychiatric patients are more impulsive than healthy subjects. Our results are similar to previous reports of patients with anxiety, affective and psychotic disorders (Belzeaux et al. 2014; Halmai and Tényi 2014; Jakuszkowiak-Wojten et al. 2015a; Jakuszkowiak-Wojten et al. 2015b; Reyes-Tovilla et al. 2015), and suggest that impulsivity is higher in patients with psychiatric disorders .

However, higher scores of impulsivity in patients than in healthy subjects can be at least partly explained by the younger age and correspondingly lower educational attainment reported in the clinical sample. Several authors have found that being younger is associated with higher impulsivity (Eysenck et al. 1985; Galvan et al. 2007; Leshem and Glicksohn 2007; Stanford et al. 1996), as well as more intense sensation seeking, which are often conflated (Steinberg et al. 2008). Conversely, as age advances, the increase in reward seeking and the structural maturation of the cognitive control system and its connections permit greater self-regulation and impulse control (Paus 2005).

We also found that there are specific risk factors such as substance use that differ between healthy subjects and psychiatric patients, which supports previous findings in the international literature in the field (Alnıak et al. 2016; Lozano et al. 2016).

When we analyzed impulsivity traits in healthy subjects by gender, no differences emerged between men and woman, as has been reported for individuals without a psychiatric disease (Muñoz et al. 2014). However, a different scenario was observed in the group of psychiatric patients. We found higher scores in the *self-control* and *spontaneous behavior* dimensions in women, as well as in the total score on Plutchik's Scale. In general, gender differences in impulsivity traits have shown mixed results.

While multiple studies suggest that males may be more impulsive than women, some authors consider that females display fluctuating levels of impulsivity depending on their cycle phase and estrogen levels (Weafer and de Wit 2014). Moreover, other studies using hypothetical delay discounting measures have found steeper discounting in women (Beck and Triplett 2009). Although gender differences in impulsivity traits have been studied in addictive disorders, borderline personality disorder and eating disorders, less information is available on disorders such as those present in the patients in this study.

Gender differences found in our study group can be partly explained by hormones, but also by the different manifestation of impairments in cognitive performance and emotional regulation between men and women. In the study by Cross et al. (2011), a major theoretical prediction for sex differences across the components of impulsivity included reward sensitivity, punishment insensitivity, and effortful control. Differences in neurobiology and brain connectivity patterns have also been found between men and women, which may be reflected in a particular behavioral manifestation or expression of a mental disorder.

One of the main findings of the present study was that, although some of the variables associated with impulsivity were similar in men and women (such as the presence of a psychiatric disorder and a younger age), other important related variables were different by gender. The main ones in men were: cocaine use, unemployment and being married and alcohol use and lower educational attainment in women.

Thus, the use of various substances predicts impulsivity by gender. These results are consistent with previous research, since impulsivity has been strongly implicated in drug use and abuse (de Wit 2009; Perry and Carroll 2008), although drug use also produces both acute and chronic changes in impulsivity (Weafer and de Wit 2014). Even though men and women may use the same drugs, frequency of use may vary and be driven by different motivations (Brady et al. 2009). Women may be more likely to engage in addictive behaviors for negative reinforcement reasons (e.g., escape from stress) whereas men may be more likely to engage in addictive behaviors for positive reinforcement reasons (e.g., seeking a high) (Mitchell and Potenza 2015). Thus, according to the last National Survey of Addictions in Mexico, an increase in cocaine use was observed in men (0.9%) (Villatoro-Velázquez et al. 2012); while the prevalence of ever using alcohol showed a higher increase in women, from 53.6% to 62.6% (Medina-Mora et al. 2012).

There was also a difference by gender regarding other important variables for impulsivity such as being unemployed and married for men. These results may have a cultural explanation and could vary in different contexts. For both men and women, unemployment is obviously a significant, stressful life event, which could trigger the onset of mental illnesses and even suicide ideation or attempts (Mucci et al. 2016), and therefore an increase in impulsivity. In Mexico, even though a similar number of men and women are economically active, unemployment could have a greater impact on men due to social expectations about their role as the main provider, particularly when they are married.

Lastly, lower educational attainment significantly contributed to impulsivity in women. This finding could be attributed to a filtering effect, whereby highly impulsive and presumably low achieving women have less opportunity than men to continue their education, at least in the Mexican context. Unfortunately, this ended up decreasing the potentially positive effect of education on the development of self-regulation and self-control in women, adding yet another social disadvantage to the long list of well-known inequities suffered by Mexican females (and probably those of similar countries).

We acknowledge the preliminary nature of these results and the limitations of our study. Interpreting the clinical significance of these findings should be done cautiously, as sample sizes were small and there could be heterogeneity. Due to the varied demographic characteristics in the sample, the gender-related differences described could be accounted for by variables not included in these analyses. Lastly, we did not test the results with other endophenotypes correlated with impulsivity.

Conclusion

In conclusion, our results show that impulsivity traits are present in patients with psychiatric disorders, while demographic and individual variables are related to its manifestation in both men and women.

Impulsivity traits are frequent predictors of suicidal behaviors and other conflicting behaviors leading to poor prognosis and a diminished quality of life. It is therefore, an important feature to be assessed in daily clinical practice, and should be the focus of future intervention strategies so that it can be reduced or managed in a creative, proactive way.

References

Alnıak I, Erkıran M, Mutlu E (2016): Substance use is a risk factor for violent behavior in male patients with bipolar disorder. *Journal of Affective Disorders* 193:89-93.

Bauer I, Meyer T, Sanches M, Zunta-Soares G, Soares J (2015): Does a history of substance abuse and illness chronicity predict increased impulsivity in bipolar disorder? *Journal of Affective Disorders* 179:142-147.

Beck R, Triplett M (2009): Test-retest reliability of a group-administered paper-pencil measure of delay discounting. *Experimental and Clinical Psychopharmacology* 17:345-355.

Belzeaux R, Correard N, Mazzola-Pomietto P, Adida M, Cermolacce M, Azorin J (2014): Affective disorders and impulsivity. *Encephale* 40:S27-32.

Bickel W, Yi R (2006): What came first? Comment on Dom et al. (2006). *Addiction* 101:291-292.

Brady K, Back S, SE. G (2009): *Women & Addiction: A Comprehensive Handbook* New York: The Guilford Press.

Cloninger C, Przybeck T, Svrakic D (1991): The Tridimensional Personality Questionnaire: U.S. normative data. *Psychological Report* 69:1047-1057.

Congdon E, Canli T (2005): The endophenotype of impulsivity: reaching consilience through behavioral, genetic, and neuroimaging approaches. *Behavioral and Cognitive Neuroscience Reviews* 4:262-281.

Cross C, Copping L, Campbell A (2011): Sex differences in impulsivity: a meta-analysis. *Psychological Bulletin* 137:97-130.

Chachamovich E, Stefanello S, Botega N, Turecki G (2009): Which are the recent clinical findings regarding the association between depression and suicide? *Revista Brasileira de Psiquiatria* 31:S18-25.

d'Acremont M, Van der Linden M (2005): Adolescent impulsivity: Findings from a community sample. *Journal of Youth and Adolescence* 34:427-435.

de Wit H (2009): Impulsivity as a determinant and consequence of drug use: a review of underlying processes. *Addiction Biology* 14:22-31.

Dom G, D'haene P, Hulstijn W, Sabbe B (2006): Impulsivity in abstinent early- and late-onset alcoholics: differences in self-report measures and a discounting task. *Addiction* 101:50-59.

Erez G, Pilver C, Potenza M (2014): Gender-related differences in the associations between sexual impulsivity and psychiatric disorders. *Journal of Psychiatric Research* 55:117-125.

Eysenck B, Pearson P, Easting G, Allsop J (1985): Age norms for impulsiveness, venturesomeness and empathy in adults, 6, 613– 619. *Personality and Individual Differences* 6:613-619.

Farley J, Kim-Spoon J (2015): Longitudinal Associations among Impulsivity, Friend Substance Use, and Adolescent Substance Use. *Journal of Addiction Research & Therapy* 6:1000220.

First M, Spitzer R, Gibbon M, Williams J (1996): *Structured Clinical Interview for DSM-IV Axis I Disorders (SCID-I), Clinician Version.* Washington, D.C.: American Psychiatric Press.

Fresan A, Robles-García R, López-Avila A, Cloninger C (2011): Personality differences according to age and sex in a Mexican sample using the

Temperament and Character Inventory-Revised. *Comprehensive Psychiatry* 52:774-779.

Galvan A, Hare T, Voss H, Glover G, Casey B (2007): Risk taking and the adolescent brain: Who is at risk? *Developmental Science* 10:F8-F14.

Galvez J, Bauer I, Sanches M, Wu H, Hamilton J, Mwangi B, et al. (2014): Shared clinical associations between obesity and impulsivity in rapid cycling bipolar disorder: a systematic review. *Journal of Affective Disorders* 168:306-313.

Halmai T, Tényi T (2014): Psychosis and violence -- literature review from a preventive point of view. *Psychiatria Hungarica* 29:35-47.

Hipwell A, Keenan K, Loeber R, Battista D (2010): Early predictors of sexually intimate behaviors in an urban sample of young girls. *Developmental Psychology* 46:366-378.

Hodgins D, Holub A (2015): Components of Impulsivity in Gambling Disorder. *International Journal of Mental Health and Addiction* 13:699-711.

Iancu I, Bodner E, Roitman S, Piccone Sapir A, Poreh A, Kotler M (2010): Impulsivity, aggression and suicide risk among male schizophrenia patients. *Psychopathology* 43:223-229.

Iancu I, Sapir A, Shaked G, Poreh A, Dannon P, Chelben J, et al. (2006): Increased suicidal risk among smoking schizophrenia patients. *Clinical Neuropharmacology* 29:230-237.

Jakuszkowiak-Wojten K, Landowski J, Wiglusz M, Cubała W (2015a): Impulsivity and Panic Disorder: an exploratory study of psychometric correlates. *Psychiatria Danubina* 27:S456-458.

Jakuszkowiak-Wojten K, Landowski J, Wiglusz M, Cubała W (2015b): Impulsivity in anxiety disorders. A critical review. *Psychiatria Danubina* 27:S452-455.

Klonsky E, May A (2010): Rethinking impulsivity in suicide. *Suicide & Life-Threatening Behavior* 40:612-619.

Leshem R, Glicksohn J (2007): The construct of impulsivity revisited. *Personality and Individual Differences* 43:681-691.

Lozano Ó, Rojas A, Fernández Calderón F (2016): Psychiatric comorbidity and severity of dependence on substance users: how it impacts on their health-related quality of life? *Journal of Mental Health* 29:1-8.

Lundahl A, Wahlstrom L, Christ C, Stoltenberg S (2015): Gender differences in the relationship between impulsivity and disordered eating behaviors and attitudes. *Eating Behaviors* 18:120-124.

Mancke F, Bertsch K, Herpertz S (2015): Gender differences in aggression of borderline personality disorder. *Borderline Personality Disorder and Emotion Dysregulation* 2:7.

Medina-Mora M, Villatoro-Velázquez J, Fleiz-Bautista C, Téllez-Rojo M, Mendoza-Alvarado L, Romero-Martínez M, et al. (2012): *Encuesta Nacional de Adicciones 2011: Reporte de Alcohol.* Ciudad de México: INPRFM, INSP, Secretaría de Salud. [*National Survey of Addictions 2011: Alcohol Report.*]

Miller J, Flory K, Lynam D, Leukefeld C (2003): A test of the four-factor model of impulsivity-related traits. *Personality and Individual Differences* 34:1403-1418.

Mitchell M, Potenza M (2014): Addictions and Personality Traits: Impulsivity and Related Constructs. *Current Behavioral Neuroscience Reports* 1:1-12.

Mitchell M, Potenza M (2015): Importance of sex differences in impulse control and addictions. *Frontiers in Psychiatry* 6:24.

Moeller F, Barratt E, Dougherty D, Schmitz J, Swann A (2001): Psychiatric aspects of impulsivity. *American Journal of Psychiatry* 158:1783-1793.

Mucci N, Giorgi G, Roncaioli M, Fiz Perez J, Arcangeli G (2016): The correlation between stress and economic crisis: a systematic review. *Neuropsychiatric Disease and Treatment* 12:983-993.

Muñoz I, Hernández M, Pedraza M, Domínguez E, Ruiz M, Isidro G, et al. (2014): Impulsivity among migraine patients: Study in a series of 155 cases. *Neurologia* S0213-4853(14)00229-1.

Ortal S, van de Glind G, Johan F, Itai B, Nir Y, Iliyan I, et al. (2015): The role of different aspects of impulsivity as independent risk factors for substance use disorders in patients with ADHD: A review. *Current Drug Abuse Reviews* 8:119-133.

Páez F, Jiménez A, López A, Raull J, Ortega-Soto H, Nicolini H (1996): Estudio de validez de la traducción al castellano de la Escala de Impulsividad de Plutchik. *Salud Mental* 19:10-12. [Study of the validity of the translation into Spanish of the Plutchik Impulsivity Scale. *Mental Health*]

Paus T (2005): Mapping brain maturation and cognitive development during adolescence. *Trends in Cognitive Sciences* 9:60-68.

Perry J, Carroll M (2008): The role of impulsive behavior in drug abuse. *Psychopharmacology* 200:1-26.

Plutchik R, Van Praag H (1989): The measurement of suicidality, aggressivity and impulsivity. *Progress in Neuro-Psychopharmacology & Biological Psychiatry* 13 Suppl:S23-34.

Reyes-Tovilla J, Hernández Yánez H, Peralta-Jiménez Y, Ramón-Frías T, Juárez-Rojop I, Pool-García S, et al. (2015): Differences between patients that made an impulsive or premeditated suicide attempt in a Mexican population. *International Journal of Psychiatry in Medicine* 49:63-74.

Sharma L, Markon K, Clark L (2014): Toward a theory of distinct types of "impulsive" behaviors: A meta-analysis of self-report and behavioral measures. *Psychological Bulletin* 140:374-408.

Spivak B, Shabash E, Sheitman B, Weizman A, Mester R (2003): The effects of clozapine versus haloperidol on measures of impulsive aggression and suicidality in chronic schizophrenia patients: an open, nonrandomized, 6-month study. *Journal of Clinical Psychiatry* 64:755-760.

Stanford M, Greve K, Boudreaux J, Mathias C, Brumbelow J (1996): Impulsiveness and risk taking behavior: Comparison of high-school and college students using the Barratt Impulsiveness Scale. *Personality and Individual Differences* 21:1073-1075.

Steinberg L, Albert D, Cauffman E, Banich M, Graham S, Woolard J (2008): Age differences in sensation seeking and impulsivity as indexed by behavior and self-report: evidence for a dual systems model. *Developmental Psychology,* 44:1764-1778.

Stoltenberg S, Batien B, Birgenheir D (2008): Does gender moderate associations among impulsivity and health-risk behaviors? *Addictive Behaviors* 33:252-265.

Swann A, Dougherty D, Pazzaglia P, Pham M, Steinberg J, Moeller F (2005): Increased impulsivity associated with severity of suicide attempt history in patients with bipolar disorder. *American Journal of Psychiatry* 162:1680-1687.

Villatoro-Velázquez J, Medina-Mora M, Fleiz-Bautista C, Téllez-Rojo M, Mendoza-Alvarado L, Romero-Martínez M, et al. (2012): *Encuesta Nacional de Adicciones 2011: Reporte de Drogas*. Ciudad de México: INPRFM, INSP, Secretaría de Salud. [*National Survey of Addictions 2011: Drug Report.*]

Watkins H, Meyer T (2013): Is there an empirical link between impulsivity and suicidality in bipolar disorders? A review of the current literature and the potential psychological implications of the relationship. *Bipolar Disorders* 15:542-558.

Weafer J, de Wit H (2014): Sex differences in impulsive action and impulsive choice. *Addictive Behaviors* 39:1573-1579.

Witte T, Gordon K, Smith P, Van Orden K (2012): Stoicism and sensation seeking: Male vulnerabilities for the acquired capability for suicide. *Journal of Research in Personality* 46:384-392.

Wrege J, Schmidt A, Walter A, Smieskova R, Bendfeldt K, Radue E, et al. (2014): Effects of cannabis on impulsivity: a systematic review of neuroimaging findings. *Current Pharmaceutical Design* 20:2126-2137.

Zhang J, Lin L (2014): The moderating effects of impulsivity on Chinese rural young suicide. *Journal of Clinical Psychology* 70:579-588.

INDEX

B

C

D

E

F

G

H

I

J

L

M

Q

R

S

T

U

V

W

Y